Editor
Jennifer Overend Prior, M. Ed.

Editorial Project Manager
Lori Kamola, M.S. Ed.

Editor-in-Chief
Sharon Coan, M.S. Ed.

Illustrator
Sue Fullam

Cover Artist
Lesley Palmer

Art Coordinator
Denice Adorno

Imaging
Alfred Lau
Temo Parra
James Edward Grace

Product Manager
Phil Garcia

Publishers
Rachelle Cracchiolo, M.S. Ed.
Mary Dupuy Smith, M.S. Ed.

LEVEL 6

NONFICTION COMPREHENSION

Test Practice

Author
Irene Gilman, Ph.D.

Introduction by Kathleen Lewis, M.A.

Project Developer
Edward Fry, Ph.D.

Reading Passages provided by
TIME FOR KIDS magazine

Teacher Created Materials

Teacher Created Materials, Inc.
6421 Industry Way
Westminster, CA 92683
www.teachercreated.com
ISBN-0-7439-3513-6
©2001 Teacher Created Materials, Inc.
Reprinted, 2001
Made in U.S.A.

Table of Contents

Introduction. 3

Lesson 1: It's Raining Monarchs. 19

Lesson 2: Raising Royal Treasure. 25

Lesson 3: Keep the Grownups Out of It 31

Lesson 4: Remembering Their Journey 37

Lesson 5: Dazzling Diamonds 43

Lesson 6: A Real Pain in the Neck 49

Lesson 7: A Million Butterflies 55

Lesson 8: Exploring the Deep 61

Lesson 9: Serious About Fun. 67

Lesson 10: Race the Wind 73

Lesson 11: Panic in Paris. 79

Lesson 12: China's Big Dam 85

Lesson 13: Should Kids Be Able to Surf the Internet?. 91

Lesson 14: The Sandia Pueblo Should Share the Land 97

Lesson 15: Tragedy in the Jungle 103

Lesson 16: Amazon Alert! 109

Lesson 17: Global Warning 115

Lesson 18: A Healthy Rise in Vaccinations 121

Lesson 19: Goal: Ending Child Labor. 127

Lesson 20: Viking Voyage. 133

Answer Key. 139

Answer Sheet 144

(**Note:** Each six-part lesson revolves around an article from *Time For Kids*. The article titles are listed here for you to choose topics that will appeal to your students, but the individual articles do not begin on the first page of the lessons. The lessons in this book may be done in any order.)

Introduction

In a day of increased accountability and standards-based instruction, teachers are feeling greater pressure for their students to perform well on standardized tests. Every teacher knows that students who can read, and comprehend what they read, will have better test performance.

In many classrooms today, teachers experience challenges they are not trained to meet, including limited English speakers, students with disabilities, high student mobility rates, and student apathy. Many states with poor standardized test scores have students that come from print-poor environments. Teachers need help developing competent readers and students who can apply their knowledge in the standardized test setting.

The *Nonfiction Comprehension Test Practice* series is a tool that will help teachers to teach comprehension skills to their students and enable their students to perform better in a test setting. This series supplies motivating, readable, interesting, nonfiction text, and comprehension exercises to help students practice comprehension skills while truly becoming better readers. The activities can be quick or in depth, allowing students to practice skills daily. What is practiced daily will be acquired by students. Practice for standardized tests needs to be started at the beginning of the school year, not a few weeks before the tests. The articles in this series are current and develop knowledge about today's world as well as the past. Students will begin thinking, talking, and developing a framework of knowledge which is crucial for comprehension.

When a teacher sparks an interest in knowledge, students will become life-long learners. In the process of completing these test practice activities, not only will you improve your students' test scores, you will create better readers and life-long learners.

━━━━━━━ Readability ━━━━━━━

All of the articles used in this series have been edited for readability. The Fry Graph, The Dale-Chall Readability Formula, or the Spache Readability Formula was used depending on the level of the article. Of more than 100 predictive readability formulas, these are the most widely used. These formulas count and factor in three variables: the number of words, syllables, and sentences. The Dale-Chall and Spache formulas also use vocabulary lists. The Dale-Chall Formula is typically used for upper-elementary and secondary grade-level materials. It uses its own vocabulary list and takes into account the total number of words and sentences. The formula reliably gives the readability for the chosen text. The Spache Formula is vocabulary-based, paying close attention to the percentage of words not present in the formula's vocabulary list. This formula is best for evaluating primary and early elementary texts. Through the use of these formulas, the levels of the articles are appropriate and comprehensible for students at each grade level.

Introduction *(cont.)*

General Lesson Plan

At each grade level of this series, there are 20 articles that prove interesting and readable to students. Each article is followed by questions on the following topics:

Sentence comprehension—Five true/false statements are related back to one sentence from the text.

Word study—One word from the text is explained (origin, part of speech, unique meaning, etc.). Activities can include completion items (cloze statements), making illustrations, or compare and contrast items.

Paragraph comprehension—This section contains one paragraph from the text and five multiple-choice questions directly related to that paragraph. The questions range from drawing information directly from the page to forming opinions and using outside knowledge.

Whole story comprehension—Eight multiple-choice questions relate back to the whole article or a major part of it. They can include comprehension that is factual, is based on opinion, involves inference, uses background knowledge, involves sequencing or classifying, relates to cause and effect, and involves understanding the author's intent. All levels of reading comprehension are covered.

Enrichment for language mechanics and expression—This section develops language mechanics and expression through a variety of activities.

Graphic development—Graphic organizers that relate to the article are used to answer a variety of comprehension questions. In some lessons, students create their own maps, graphs, and diagrams that relate to the article.

The following is a list of words from the lessons that may be difficult for some students. These words are listed here so that you may review them with your students as needed.

Word	Page	Word	Page
Monarch	19	Holocaust	55
subordinate	23	sanctuaries	63
Cleopatra	25	Archibutyrophobia	83
Ptolemy	27	Melghat	105
orthopedic	49		

Introduction _(cont.)_

What Do Students Need to Learn?

Successful reading requires comprehension. Comprehending means having the ability to connect words and thoughts to knowledge already possessed. If you have little or no knowledge of a subject, it is difficult to comprehend an article or text written on that subject. Comprehension requires motivation and interest. Once your students start acquiring knowledge, they will want to fill in the gaps and learn more.

In order to help students be the best readers they can be, a teacher needs to be familiar with what students need to know to comprehend well. A teacher needs to know Bloom's levels of comprehension, traditional comprehension skills and expected products, and the types of questions that are generally used on standardized comprehension tests, as well as methods that can be used to help students to build a framework for comprehension.

Bloom's Taxonomy

In 1956, Benjamin Bloom created a classification for questions that are commonly used to demonstrate comprehension. These levels are listed here along with the corresponding skills that will demonstrate understanding and are important to remember when teaching comprehension to assure that students have attained higher levels of comprehension. Use this classification to form your own questions whenever students read or listen to literature.

Knowledge—Students will recall information. They will show knowledge of dates, events, places, and main ideas. Questions will include words such as: who, what, where, when, list, identify, and name.

Comprehension—Students will understand information. They will compare and contrast, order, categorize, and predict consequences. Questions will include words such as: compare, contrast, describe, summarize, predict, and estimate.

Application—Students will use information in new situations. Questions will include words such as: apply, demonstrate, solve, classify, and complete.

Analysis—Students will see patterns. They will be able to organize parts and figure out meaning. Questions will include words such as: order, explain, arrange, and analyze.

Synthesis—Students will use old ideas to create new ones. They will generalize, predict, and draw conclusions. Questions will include words such as: what if?, rewrite, rearrange, combine, create, and substitute.

Evaluation—Students will compare ideas and assess value. They will make choices and understand a subjective viewpoint. Questions will include words such as: assess, decide, and support your opinion.

Introduction (cont.)

Comprehension Skills

There are many skills that form the complex activity of comprehension. This wide range of understandings and abilities develops over time in competent readers. The following list includes many traditional skills found in scope and sequence charts and standards for reading comprehension.

identifies details

recognizes stated main idea

follows directions

determines sequence

recalls details

locates reference

recalls gist of story

labels parts

summarizes

recognizes anaphoric relationships

identifies time sequence

describes a character

retells story in own words

infers main idea

infers details

infers cause and effect

infers authors purpose/intent

classifies, places into categories

compares and contrasts

draws conclusions

makes generalizations

recognizes paragraph (text) organization

predicts outcome

recognizes hyperbole and exaggeration

experiences empathy for a character

experiences an emotional reaction to the text

judges quality/appeal of text

judges author's qualifications

recognizes facts vs. opinions

applies understanding to a new situation

recognizes literary style

recognizes figurative language

identifies mood

identifies plot and story line

Introduction *(cont.)*

Observable Comprehension Products

There are many exercises that students can complete when they comprehend the material they read. Some of these products can be performed orally in small groups. Some lend themselves more to independent paper-and-pencil type activities. Although there are more, the following are common and comprehensive products of comprehension.

Recognizing—underlining, multiple choice items, matching, true/false statements

Recalling—writing a short answer, filling in the blanks, flashcard question and answer

Paraphrasing—retelling in own words, summarizing

Classifying—grouping components, naming clusters, completing comparison tables, ordering components on a scale

Following directions—completing steps in a task, using a recipe, constructing

Visualizing—graphing, drawing a map, illustrating, making a time line, creating a flow chart

Fluent reading—accurate pronunciation, phrasing, intonation, dramatic qualities

Reading Comprehension Questions

Teaching the kinds of questions that appear on standardized tests gives students the framework to anticipate and thus look for the answers to questions while reading. This framework will not only help students' scores, but it will actually help them learn how to comprehend what they are reading. Some of the types of questions students will find on standardized comprehension tests are as follows:

Vocabulary—These questions are based on word meaning, common words, proper nouns, technical words, geographical words, and unusual adjectives.

Facts—These questions ask exactly what was written, using who, what, when, where, why, how, and how many.

Sequence—These questions are based on order—what happened first, last, and in between.

Conditionals—These questions use qualifying terms such as: if, could, alleged, etc.

Summarizing—These questions require students to restate, choose main ideas, conclude, and create a new title. Also important here is for students to understand and state the author's purpose.

Outcomes—These questions often involve readers drawing upon their own experiences or bringing outside knowledge to the composition. Students must understand cause and effect, results of actions, and implications.

Opinion—These questions ask the author's intent and mood and require use of background knowledge to answer.

Introduction *(cont.)*

Reading and comprehension can be easier for students with a few simple practices. For top comprehension, students need a wide vocabulary, ideas about the subject they are reading, and understanding of the structure of the text. Pre-reading activities will help students in all of these areas. Graphic organizers help students build vocabulary, brainstorm ideas, and understand the structure of the text.

Graphic organizers aid students with vocabulary and comprehension. Graphic organizers can help students comprehend more and, in turn, gain insight into how to comprehend in future readings. This process teaches a student a way to connect new information to prior knowledge that is stored in his or her brain. Different types of graphic organizers are listed below by category.

Concept organizers include: semantic maps, spider maps (word webs), Venn diagrams, and fishbone diagrams.

Semantic map—This organizer builds vocabulary. A word for study is placed in the center of the page, and four categories are made around it. The categories expand on the nature of the word and relate it back to personal knowledge and experience of the students.

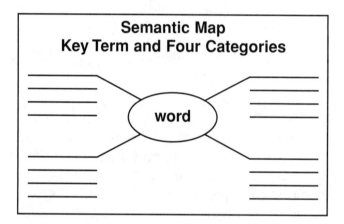

Spider map (word web)—The topic, concept, or theme is placed in the middle of the page. Like a spider's web, thoughts and ideas come out from the center, beginning with main ideas and flowing out to details.

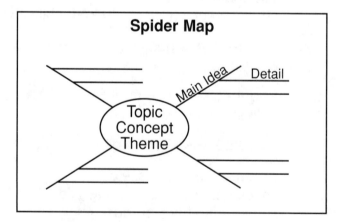

Introduction *(cont.)*

Venn diagram—This organizer compares and contrasts two ideas. With two large circles intersecting, each circle represents a different topic. The area of each circle that does not intersect is for ideas and concepts that are only true about one topic. The intersection is for ideas and concepts that are true about both topics.

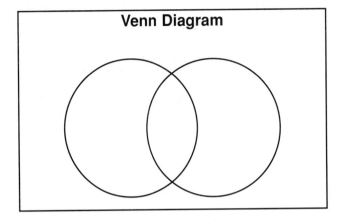

Fishbone diagram—This organizer deals with cause and effect. The result is listed first, branching out in a fishbone pattern with the causes that lead up to the result, along with other effects that happened along the way.

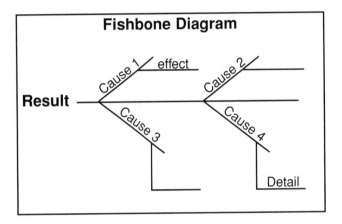

Continuum organizers can be linear or circular and contain a chain of events. These include time lines, chain of events, multiple linear maps, and circular or repeating maps.

Time lines—Whether graphing ancient history or the last hour, time lines help students to see how events have progressed and understand patterns in history.

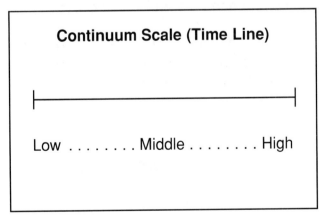

Introduction (cont.)

Chain of Events—This organizer not only shows the progression of time but also emphasizes cause and effect. Beginning with the initiating event inside of a box, subsequent arrows and boxes follow showing the events in order.

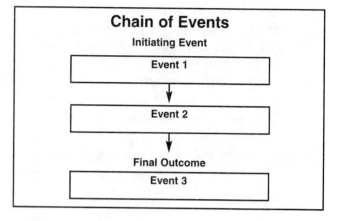

Multiple linear maps—These organizers can help students visualize how different events can be happening at the same time, either in history or in a story, and how those events affect each other.

Circular or repeating maps—These organizers lend themselves to events that happen in a repeating pattern like events in science, such as the water cycle.

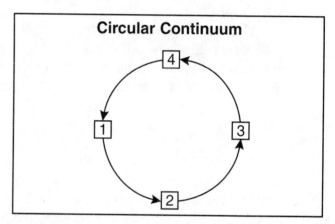

Hierarchical organizers show structure. These include: network trees, structured overviews, and class/example and properties maps. These organizers help students begin to visualize and comprehend hierarchy of knowledge, going from the big picture to the details.

Network tree—This organizer begins with a main, general topic. From there it branches out to examples of that topic, further branching out with more and more detail.

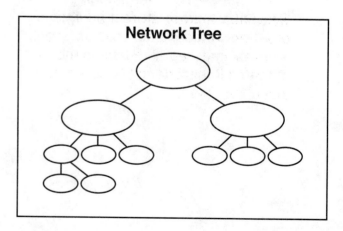

Introduction (cont.)

Structured overview—This is very similar to a network tree, but it varies in that it has a very structured look.

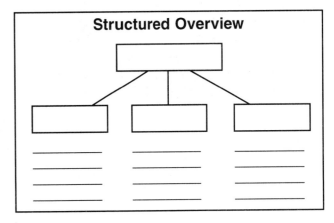

Class/example and properties map—Organized graphically, this map gives the information of class, example, and properties.

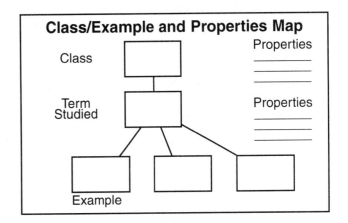

Spreadsheets are important organizers today. Much computer information is stored on spreadsheets. It is important for students to learn how to create, read, and comprehend these organizers. These include semantic feature analysis, compare and contrast matrices, and simple spreadsheet tables.

Semantic feature analysis—This organizer gives examples of a topic and lists features. A plus or a minus indicates if that example possesses those features.

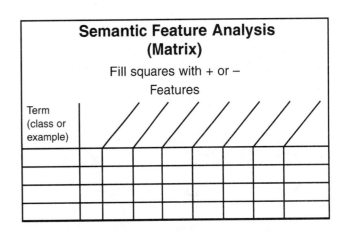

═══════════════════ *Graphic Organizers (cont.)* ═══════════════════

Compare and contrast matrix—This organizer compares and contrasts two or more examples on different attributes.

Compare/Contrast Matrix (Spreadsheets)		
Attribute 1		
Attribute 2		
Attribute 3		

Simple spreadsheet table—Much information can be visualized through spreadsheets or tables. Choose examples and qualities and arrange them in spreadsheet style.

Maps are helpful in understanding spatial relationships. There are geographical maps, but there are also street maps and floor plans.

Geographical map—These organizers can range from globes to cities and details are limited.

Street map—Information on this type of organizer becomes more detailed.

Floor plan—This organizer becomes more detailed, from a building to a room or a student's desk.

Numerical graphs such as bar graphs, pie charts, and tables become important in comprehension, too.

Bar graph—With a vertical and a horizontal axis, this graph shows a comparison between subjects. It is important to be able to draw the correct information out of it.

Pie chart—In the circular shape of a pie, amounts totaling 100% are shown as pieces of pie. Once again, drawing correct information is important.

Using graphic organizers while reading class material will help students know what to do in order to better comprehend material on standardized comprehension tests. Further, a varied use of all types of organizers will help students of different learning styles hit a method that works for them.

═══════════════════ Pre-reading Strategies ═══════════════════

It is widely understood that for comprehension and acquisition to take place, new information must be integrated with what the reader knows. Pre-reading strategies will help students to build knowledge and restructure the information they already possess in order to more fully comprehend what they are reading. After a teacher has spent time teaching pre-reading strategies, students will know what to do when reading on their own.

Introduction (cont.)

Building Vocabulary

Common sense reveals that there is a symbiotic relationship between knowledge of vocabulary and comprehension. Vocabulary development and comprehension span the curriculum. Students come across a large and diverse vocabulary in science, social science, mathematics, art, and even physical education. Skills and strategies for understanding vocabulary can be taught throughout the day. You can build your students' vocabulary directly and/or indirectly. Both ways have shown merit for different learners, so a combination will be sure to help all of the learners in your classroom.

Whether done directly or indirectly, teaching the kind of vocabulary that occurs in a text will greatly improve comprehension. Teaching vocabulary directly, a teacher would list the vocabulary in the text and have the students find the definitions in some manner. Indirectly, a teacher would introduce the content of the text and then elicit vocabulary that the students bring with them on the subject. The use of graphic organizers is helpful in doing this. (See page 8 for different types.) The teacher would lead the discussion to specific words if necessary.

Direct teaching—The more conventional way of teaching vocabulary has its merits. Give students a list of vocabulary words and they look them up. This way teaches the use of reference materials and for some learners it is a good way to learn vocabulary. However, students truly learn vocabulary when they are involved in the construction of meaning rather than simply memorizing definitions.

Incidental or indirect teaching—This is really a combination of direct teaching and incidental learning for the well-equipped teacher. Teaching in this fashion, a teacher uses the students' knowledge and interests to begin a vocabulary development session that will end with what he or she wants the students to learn. Along the way, the teacher builds a grand vocabulary list and student interest. Also, students buy into the fact that they are part of the process and that learning vocabulary can be a personal experience that they can control. The students will learn how to become independent learners, studying things that interest them.

A general approach to building vocabulary could include the following:

Semantic association—Students brainstorm a list of words associated with a familiar word, sharing everyone's knowledge of vocabulary and discussing the less familiar words.

Semantic mapping—Once the brainstorming is done, students can group the words into categories, creating a visual organization to understand relationships.

Semantic feature analysis—Another way to group words is according to certain features. Use a chart to show similarities and differences between words.

Analogies—This practice will further help students to see the relationships of words. Also, analogies are often used on standardized tests. (e.g., Doctor is to patient as teacher is to _student_.)

Word roots and origins—The study of these, as well as affixes, will help students to deduce new words. Students can ask themselves, "Does it look like a word I know? Can I figure out the meaning in the given context?"

Introduction *(cont.)*

Synonyms and antonyms—The study of these related words provides a structure for meaning and is also good practice for learning and building vocabulary.

Brainstorming—The use of graphic organizers to list and categorize ideas will help greatly with comprehension. A great way to get started is with a KWL chart. By listing ideas that are known, what students want to know, and, when finished, what they learned, relationships will be established so that comprehension and acquisition of knowledge will take place. Word webs work well, too. Anticipating the types of words and ideas that will appear in the text will help with fluency of reading as well as with comprehension.

========= **Understanding Structure** =========

To be able to make predictions and find information in writing, a student must understand structure. From the structure of a sentence to a paragraph to an essay, this skill is important and sometimes overlooked in instruction. Some students have been so immersed in literature that they have a natural understanding of structure. For instance, they know that a fairy tale starts out "Once upon a time . . . ," has a good guy and a bad guy, has a problem with a solution, and ends ". . . happily ever after." But when a student does not have this prior knowledge, making heads or tails of a fairy tale is difficult. The same holds true with not understanding that the first sentence of a paragraph will probably contain the main idea, followed with examples of that idea. When looking back at a piece to find the answer to a question, understanding structure will allow students to quickly scan the text for the correct area in which to find the information. Furthermore, knowing where a text is going to go structurally will help prediction as well as comprehension.

Building a large vocabulary is important for comprehension, but comprehension and acquisition also require a framework for relating new information to what is already in the brain. Students must be taught the structure of sentences and paragraphs. Knowing the structure of these, they will begin to anticipate and predict what will come next. Not having to decode every word reduces the time spent reading a sentence and thus helps students remember what they read at the beginning of the sentence. Assessing an author's purpose and quickly recalling a graphic or framework of personal knowledge will help a reader predict and anticipate what vocabulary and ideas might come up in an article or story.

Several activities will help with understanding structure. The following list offers some ideas to help students:

Write—A great way to understand structure is to use it. Teach students the proper structure when they write.

Color code—When reading a text, students can use colored pencils or crayons to color code certain elements such as main idea, supporting sentences, and details. Once the colors are in place, they can study and tell in their own words about paragraph structure.

Introduction (cont.)

Understanding Structure (cont.)

Go back in the text—Discuss a comprehension question with students. Ask them, "What kinds of words are you going to look for in the text to find the answer? Where are you going to look for them?" (The students should pick main ideas in the question and look for those words in the topic sentences of the different paragraphs.)

Graphic organizers—Use the list of graphic organizers (page 8) to find one that will suit your text. Have students create an organizer as a class, in a small group, or with a partner.

Study common order—Students can also look for common orders. Types of orders can include chronological, serial, logical, functional, spatial, and hierarchical.

Standardized Tests

Standardized tests have taken a great importance in education today. As an educator, you know that standardized tests do not necessarily provide an accurate picture of a student. There are many factors that do not reflect the students' competence that sway the results of these tests.

- The diversity of our big country makes the tests difficult to norm.
- Students that are talented in areas other than math and language cannot show this talent.
- Students who do not speak and read English fluently will not do well on standardized tests.
- Students who live in poverty do not necessarily have the experiences necessary to comprehend the questions.

The list could go on, but there does have to be some sort of assessment of progress that a community can use to decide how the schools are doing. Standardized tests and their results are receiving more and more attention these days. The purpose of this series, along with creating better readers, is to help students get better results on standardized tests.

Test Success

The ability to do well when taking traditional standardized tests on comprehension requires at least three things:

- a large vocabulary of sight words
- the mastery of certain specific test-taking skills
- the ability to recognize and control stress

Vocabulary has already been discussed in detail. Test-taking skills and recognizing and controlling stress can be taught and will be discussed in this section.

Introduction *(cont.)*

Every student in your class needs good test-taking skills, and almost all of them will need to be taught these skills. Even fluent readers and extremely logical students will fair better on standardized tests if they are taught a few simple skills for taking tests.

These test-taking skills are:

- The ability to follow complicated and sometimes confusing directions. Teach students to break down the directions and translate them into easy, understandable words. Use this series to teach them the types of questions that will appear.

- The ability to scale back what they know and concentrate on just what is asked and what is contained in the text—show them how to restrict their responses. Question students on their answers when doing practice exercises and have them show where they found the answer in the text.

- The ability to rule out confusing distracters in multiple choice answers. Teach students to look for key words and match up the information from the text.

- The ability to maintain concentration during boring and tedious repetition. Use practice time to practice this and reward students for maintaining concentration. Explain to students why they are practicing and why their concentration is important for the day of the test.

There are also environmental elements that you can practice with throughout the year in order for your students to become more accustomed to them for the testing period.

If your desks are pushed together, have students move them apart so they will be accustomed to the feel on test-taking day.

- Put a "Testing—Do Not Disturb" sign on the door.

- Require "test etiquette" when practicing: no talking, attentive listening, and following directions.

- Provide a strip of construction paper for each student to use as a marker.

- Establish a routine for replacing broken pencils. Give each student two sharpened pencils and have a back-up supply ready. Tell students they will need to raise their broken pencil in their hand, and you will give them a new one. One thing students should not worry about is the teacher's reaction to a broken pencil.

- Read the instructions to the students as you would when giving a standardized test so they grow accustomed to your test-giving voice.

- As a teacher, you probably realize that what is practiced daily is what is best learned. All of these practices work well to help students improve their scores.

Introduction *(cont.)*

Reduce Stress and Build Confidence

As well as the physical and mental aspects of test-taking, there is also the psychological. It is important to reduce students' stress and increase students' confidence during the year.

- In order to reduce stress, it first needs to be recognized. Discuss feelings and apprehensions about testing. Give students some tools for handling stress.

- Begin talking about good habits at the beginning of the year. Talk about getting enough sleep, eating a good breakfast, and exercising before and after school. Consider sending home a letter encouraging parents to start these good routines with their children at home.

- Explain the power of positive thought to your students. Tell them to use their imaginations to visualize themselves doing well. Let them know that they have practiced all year and are ready for what is to come.

- Remember to let students stretch and walk around between tests. Try using "Simon Says" with younger students throughout the year to get them to breathe deeply, stretch, and relax so it won't be a novel idea during test time.

- Build confidence during the year when using the practice tests. Emphasize that these tests are for learning. If they could get all of the answers right the first time, they wouldn't need any practice. Encourage students to state at least one thing they learned from doing the practice test.

- Give credit for reasonable answers. Explain to students that the test makers write answers that seem almost true to really test the students' understanding. Encourage students to explain why they chose the answers they gave, and then reason with the whole class on how not to be duped the next time.

- Promote a relaxed, positive outlook on test-taking. Let your students know on the real day that they are fully prepared to do their best.

Introduction *(cont.)*

Suggestions for the Teacher

When practicing skills for comprehension, it is important to vocalize and discuss the process in finding an answer. After building vocabulary, tapping background knowledge, and discussing the structure that might be used in the article, have the students read the article. If they are not able to read the article independently, have them read with a partner or in a small teacher-lead group. After completing these steps, work through the comprehension questions. The following are suggestions for working through these activities.

- Have students read the text silently and answer the questions.

- Have students correct their own papers.

- Discuss each answer and how the students came to their answers.

- Refer to the exact wording in the text.

- Discuss whether students had to tap their own knowledge or not.

Answer Sheet

The teacher can choose to use the blank answer sheet located at the back of the book for practice filling in bubble forms for standardized tests. The rows have not been numbered so that the teacher can use the form for any test, filling in the numbers and copying for the class as necessary. The teacher can also have the students write the answers directly on the pages of the test practice sheets instead of using the bubble sheet.

Summary

Teachers need to find a way to blend test preparation with the process of learning and discovery. It is important for students to learn test-taking skills and strategies because they will be important throughout life. It is more important for students to build vocabulary and knowledge, to create frameworks for comprehension, and to become fluent readers.

The *Nonfiction Comprehension Test Practice* series is an outstanding program to start your students in the direction of becoming better readers and test-takers. These are skills they will need throughout life. Provide an atmosphere of the joy of learning and create a climate for curiosity within your classroom. With daily practice of comprehension skills and test-taking procedures, teaching comprehension may seem just a little bit easier.

Sentence Comprehension

Directions: Read the following sentence carefully and answer the questions below "True" (T) or "False" (F).

Each August, millions of monarch butterflies begin to migrate from Canada and the northern U.S. to spend the winter in the sunny south.

---

1. Butterflies migrate from Canada to the northern United States. _____

2. Monarch butterflies begin their migration in the summer. _____

3. Migration means to morph, or to change. _____

4. Monarch butterflies, like some birds, head south for the winter. _____

5. Monarch butterflies cannot tolerate cold weather. _____

Word Study

Directions: Read the information given below and use it to answer the following questions "True" (T) or "False" (F).

Monarch

A *monarch* is a hereditary ruler such as a king or queen. Sometimes a monarch is not a king or queen, but someone or something that holds a dominant or important position. Monarch is a word made up of two parts. The first part of this word, *mono-*, means one. The second part of this word, *-arch*, means to rule or to be first.

---

1. A monarch must always be a man. _____

2. A monarch must always be a person. _____

3. A monotone sings only one note. _____

4. Part of the word oligarchy has to do with ruling. _____

5. A woman could be a monarch. _____

Paragraph Comprehension

Directions: Read the paragraph below and answer the following questions.

Despite 1999's huge migration, experts worry about the monarch butterfly's future. Loggers in Mexico have cut down some of the forests where millions of monarchs spend the winter. Farmers use weed killers that can destroy milkweed plants, the monarch's favorite food as well as its egg-laying spot. Also, the monarchs are always subject to local weather conditions. A dry spell in Texas during the summer of 1999 meant fewer plants there for the monarchs to eat.

1. The future of the monarch butterfly depends on
   a. rainfall.
   b. availability of food.
   c. a safe place to lay eggs.
   d. all of the above

2. Farmers are using weed killers to
   a. destroy the monarch butterfly.
   b. keep their crops healthy.
   c. kill butterfly eggs.
   d. get rid of the forests.

3. The term *dry spell* means
   a. drought conditions.
   b. fewer plants.
   c. lack of rain.
   d. both a and c

4. The future of monarch butterflies
   a. depends only on the farmers of Mexico.
   b. is uncertain.
   c. looks bright.
   d. is destined for extinction.

5. A monarch butterfly's favorite food is
   a. milkweed.
   b. trees.
   c. loggers.
   d. its own eggs.

Whole Story Comprehension

Directions: Read the story below and answer the questions on the following page.

It's Raining Monarchs

Have you ever seen more than 25,000 butterflies in one spot? In the fall of 1999, people in Cape May, New Jersey, were delighted by that spectacle. Fluttering clouds of monarch butterflies flew through the seaside town on their long journey south. Monarchs can fly 1,000 miles on a cold day!

Karen Oberhauser of the University of Minnesota's department of ecology thinks fair weather helped the monarchs in 1999. Milkweed plants, which monarchs eat, grew like crazy in the upper Midwest, where there was plenty of rain.

Monarchs have a wondrous life cycle. Every spring, the monarchs that have spent the winter sleeping in the south wake up and begin to fly north. Along the way, females each lay up to 7,000 eggs on the underside of milkweed plants; then they die.

In about a month, the eggs grow into striped caterpillars, which turn into adult butterflies. This generation lives only about two months and females lay more eggs. The adult butterflies that grow from these eggs fly north, where they too will lay eggs. Monarchs born in late summer live as long as nine months, which gives them time to make the journey south. In the fall, monarchs migrate south to California and Mexico.

Despite 1999's huge migration, experts worry about the monarch's future. Loggers in Mexico have cut down some of the forests where millions of monarchs spend the winter. Farmers use weed killers that can destroy milkweed plants, the monarch's favorite food as well as its egg-laying spot. Also, the monarchs are always subject to local weather conditions. A dry spell in Texas during the summer of 1999 meant fewer plants there for the monarchs to eat.

Jeffrey Glassberg, president of the North American Butterfly Association, says protecting the butterflies is worth the effort because they are such pleasant natural neighbors: "They get along well with people, are easily approachable, don't need miles of wilderness, and they add beauty and variety to people's lives."

Whole Story Comprehension (cont.)

Directions: After you have read the story on the previous page, answer the questions below.

1. Milkweed

   a. is a rare plant on which butterflies feed.

   b. is a weed that grows only in Mexico.

   c. requires ample rainfall to thrive.

   d. is the only nutritional source for a monarch butterfly.

2. Which butterflies have the longest life span?

   a. butterflies that emerge in August

   b. butterflies that lay eggs

   c. striped butterflies

   d. butterflies that emerge in April

3. Monarch butterflies migrate in the fall because

   a. they cannot live in cold temperatures.

   b. they cannot fly on a cold day.

   c. there isn't enough food in the north.

   d. both a and c

4. Which sentence is true?

   a. Cape May has an insect problem.

   b. Logging is illegal in Mexico.

   c. Jeffrey Glassberg is interested in monarch butterflies.

   d. Monarch butterflies are on the endangered species list.

5. With what do you think Jeffrey Glassberg is most concerned?

   a. watering milkweed during droughts

   b. preserving the natural habitat of the monarch butterfly

   c. changing the migratory route of the monarch butterfly

   d. people who keep butterflies as pets

6. The best definition for *migrate* is

   a. travel.

   b. change.

   c. escape.

   d. life cycle.

7. Which statement is false?

   a. Weather affects the monarch butterfly population.

   b. The life span of a monarch butterfly depends on when it first starts to live.

   c. Deforestation does not affect the monarch butterflies.

   d. A butterfly is an insect.

8. The title "It's Raining Monarchs" probably refers to

   a. the great number of monarchs that migrate.

   b. the spring rain that helps the milkweed grow.

   c. caterpillars falling from the trees.

   d. butterflies falling from the sky.

Enrichment

Directions: Read the information below and use it to answer the following questions.

In English grammar there are two types of clauses—main clauses and subordinate (or dependent) clauses. Main clauses are complete sentences that can stand by themselves. But dependent clauses cannot stand alone. They must lean or depend on a main clause. Clauses must always have a subject and a predicate, even dependent clauses.

One type of dependent clause is an adjective clause, a group of words with a subject and a predicate that acts like an adjective. But finding the subject of an adjective clause can sometimes be difficult because these clauses are introduced by a group of words called relative pronouns, such as *who, whom, that, what,* and *which*.

For example, "The pencil is on the desk. The pencil is Harry's." We can combine these two sentences by using a dependent clause: "The pencil that is Harry's is on the desk." The dependent clause is "that is Harry's."

Sometimes the relative pronoun introduces the adjective clause and sometimes it serves as the subject of the adjective clause. Note the difference between these two sentences.

> *The kick that brought the crowd to its feet broke the tie score.*

> *The soccer player whose leg is broken has to be removed from the game.*

In the first adjective clause, "that" is the subject of "brought." In the second, "whose" introduces the adjective clause.

Carefully read these sentences. Mark the sentences that have adjective clauses in them as "Yes" (Y) and those that do not as "No" (N). Before you can find the adjective clause, it might be necessary to find the subject and predicate of the main clause.

1. Milkweed plants grew like crazy in the upper Midwest. _____

2. Milkweed plants which monarchs eat grew like crazy in the upper Midwest. _____

3. The adult butterflies that grow from these eggs fly north. _____

4. The adult butterflies fly north. _____

5. Every spring, the monarchs that have spent the winter sleeping in the south wake up. _____

6. Every spring, the monarchs wake up and begin to fly north. _____

7. A dry spell in Texas during the summer of 1999 meant fewer plants. _____

8. A dry spell in Texas meant fewer plants. _____

9. Monarchs born in late summer live as long as nine months, which gives them time to make the journey south. _____

10. Monarchs born in late summer live as long as nine months. _____

Graphic Development

Directions: Look carefully at the map and tell if the statements below are "True" (T) or "False" (F).

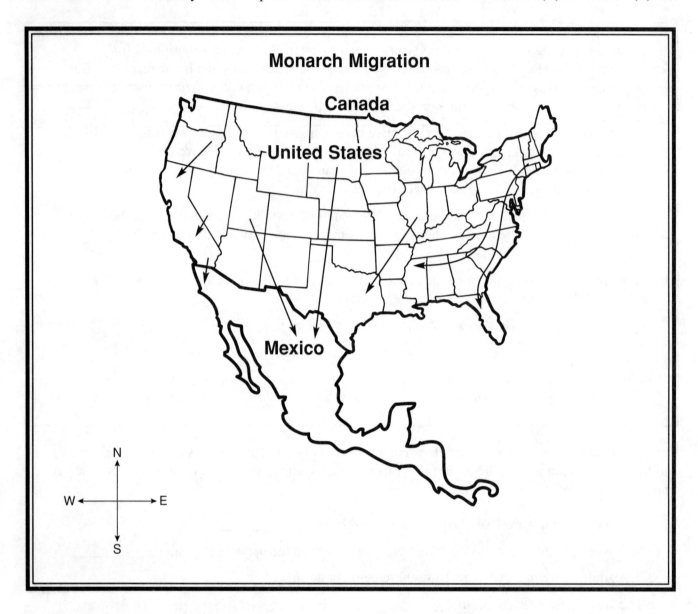

1. The same butterflies that fly south in the fall make the return journey in the spring. _____

2. The butterflies on the west coast travel to Florida. _____

3. Midwestern monarchs are affected by logging in Mexico. _____

4. Monarch butterflies begin their southern journey in Canada. _____

5. Monarch butterflies lay their eggs in the United States. _____

Sentence Comprehension

Directions: Read the sentence carefully and use it to answer the following questions "True" (T) or "False" (F).

> Though her reign ended 2,000 years ago, Cleopatra continues to enchant people everywhere.

1. Cleopatra ruled Egypt while George Washington was president of the United States. _____

2. To enchant means to interest. _____

3. Cleopatra is a fictional character. _____

4. Cleopatra is still the queen of Egypt. _____

5. Cleopatra was a ruler. _____

Word Study

Directions: Read the information given below and use it to answer the following questions "True" (T) or "False" (F).

Roman Numerals

The ancient Romans did not use the Arabic numbers that we commonly use today. If you hold up your right hand and separate your thumb from the rest of your fingers, you will see a V. The Romans used V for the number 5. Instead of writing 2, they wrote II, and instead of 3, they wrote III. But when they needed to write 4, they placed a I in front of the V or 5 and wrote IV. For 10, they wrote X. For 9, they wrote IX. For 50, they used L. For 70, they wrote LXX, but for 40, they wrote XL. For 100, they used C. For 90, they wrote XC. For 1,000, they wrote M. To write Roman numerals, you do not need to know many letter symbols, but you need to know when to place the letter symbols in front and when to place them in back of the other letters.

Today, we find Roman numerals engraved on the cornerstones of a building to tell us when the building was erected. A building put up in 2001 would have MMI written on its cornerstone, but a building put up in 1999 would have CMXCIX written on its cornerstone. Sometimes when a boy has the same name as his father and his grandfather, he is called John Smith III to show that he is the third person with this name.

1. John Smith IV is the third person in his family with this name. _____

2. A building whose cornerstone has MM on it was built in the year 1000. _____

3. XIV is the Roman way of writing 14. _____

4. XXC is the Roman way of writing 30. _____

5. XXC is the Roman way of writing 90. _____

Paragraph Comprehension

Directions: Read the paragraph below and answer the following questions.

Although the city of Alexandria still exists today, floods and earthquakes buried Antirhodos under water more than 1,600 years ago. But it wasn't lost for good. In 1996, undersea explorer Franck Goddio found this island beneath just 18 feet of water off the shore of Alexandria. He found statues, columns, pavement, and pottery buried in layers of mud, seaweed, and garbage. These were the ruins of Cleopatra's palace.

1. Cleopatra's palace was underwater

    a. for protection.

    b. due to catastrophes.

    c. because she was a mermaid.

    d. after a war.

2. Alexandria and Antirhodos were

    a. both destroyed by earthquakes.

    b. home to Cleopatra.

    c. neighboring cities in Egypt.

    d. Cleopatra's sisters.

3. Ruins are

    a. valuables that have been lost.

    b. antiques.

    c. remains of a building or town.

    d. things found underwater.

4. In this paragraph, "it" refers to

    a. Alexandria.

    b. Antirhodos.

    c. the pottery.

    d. the floods.

5. Do people still live on the island of Antirhodos?

    a. No, they do not.

    b. Yes, but only a few.

    c. Yes, there's a museum on it.

    d. No, it's never been located.

Whole Story Comprehension

Directions: Read the story below and answer the questions on the following page.

Raising Royal Treasure

It's a tale full of romance, sneaky tricks, tragedy, and most of all, girl power. Plus, it's all true. The real-life story of Cleopatra, a beautiful 17-year-old girl when she became the powerful ruler of ancient Egypt, has fascinated people for thousands of years. Now new information about Cleopatra's life is coming to the surface. Parts of her ancient royal court have been found near Alexandria, Egypt. All of these ruins are underwater.

Ancient Egyptian writings and drawings show that Cleopatra owned a royal palace on an island named Antirhodos (An-teer-uh-dose). The island was near Alexandria, the capital city of Egypt during Cleopatra's reign in the first century B.C.

Although the city of Alexandria still exists today, floods and earthquakes buried Antirhodos under water more than 1,600 years ago. But it wasn't lost for good. In 1996, undersea explorer Franck Goddio found it beneath just 18 feet of water, off the shore of Alexandria. He found statues, columns, pavement, and pottery buried in layers of mud, seaweed, and garbage. These were the ruins of Cleopatra's palace.

Cleopatra and her brother Ptolemy XIII began to rule Egypt together in 51 B.C. In keeping with royal custom, the brother and sister were married! But Ptolemy did not want to share the throne, and he forced Cleopatra out of the palace.

The quick-witted young woman saw her chance to regain power when Rome's main leader, Julius Caesar (See-zer), traveled to Egypt. In order to meet with him, Cleopatra is said to have sneaked into the palace rolled up in a carpet! Caesar soon fell in love with Cleopatra. He helped her push Ptolemy aside and take control of Egypt.

After Caesar was murdered by his enemies, a new Roman leader, Mark Antony, met Cleopatra. Just like Caesar before him, Antony fell in love with her. He moved into Cleopatra's palace at Antirhodos.

Soon people back in Rome feared that Antony was more interested in Egypt than in his own empire. They turned against him and Egypt and sent a huge army by sea, which eventually defeated Egypt. In despair, Cleopatra and Antony took their own lives. Ancient Egypt's last queen died at the age of 39.

Though her reign ended 2,000 years ago, Cleopatra continues to enchant people everywhere. For that reason, Goddio hopes to set up an underwater museum at the palace site. Visitors would be able to explore and experience Cleopatra's world up close. "To be there, underwater where she reigned and died," says Goddio, "is unbelievable."

Whole Story Comprehension (cont.)

Directions: After you have read the story on the previous page, answer the questions below.

1. How many men fell in love with Cleopatra?

   a. four

   b. two

   c. three

   d. five

2. If Antirhodos disappeared over 1,600 years ago, how did Franck Goddio know it existed?

   a. He only knew after he found it.

   b. Old maps and writings showed the location.

   c. Folktales mentioned it.

   d. Ancestors of Cleopatra told him.

3. In the last paragraph, which word below could not take the place of "enchant" without changing the meaning of the sentence?

   a. charm

   b. captivate

   c. delight

   d. encircle

4. Who helped Cleopatra regain power after Ptolemy XIII forced her off her throne?

   a. Mark Antony

   b. The ruler of Rome

   c. Julius Caesar

   d. a and b

   e. b and c

5. The Nile is the major river in Egypt. Why is Cleopatra known as the Queen of the Nile?

   a. She ruled Egypt.

   b. She was buried in the Nile.

   c. Cleopatra liked to sail.

   d. She was Queen of the Nile after Julius Caeser died.

6. What is the best substitute for the word "reign"?

   a. a royal rule

   b. a life

   c. a fall from power

7. Give the proper sequence for the following events:

   1. Antirhodos is destroyed by floods and earthquakes.

   2. Julius Caesar helps Cleopatra regain her rule of Egypt.

   3. Cleopatra and Ptolemy XIII rule Egypt.

   4. Mark Antony and Cleopatra fall in love.

   The proper sequence of events is

   a. 2, 3, 4, 1

   b. 3, 2, 4, 1

   c. 1, 2, 3, 4

   d. 3, 4, 2, 1

8. In paragraph five, the writer says Cleopatra is "said to have" sneaked into Caesar's palace. What do those words mean?

   a. People talked about it for a long time.

   b. The story is definitely not true.

   c. The story may not be true.

   d. Cleopatra told everyone her plan.

Enrichment

Directions: Read the information below and use it to answer the following questions.

In the English language, verbs have two voices: active and passive. In the active voice, the grammatical subject of the sentence is the "doer" of the action. "Mary kicked the soccer ball." In the passive voice, the grammatical subject of the sentence is the "receiver" of the action: "The soccer ball was kicked by Mary." We say "grammatical subject" because we know that Mary is the real "doer" in this sentence; Mary is the "real" subject. Sentences using the active voice are much more forceful and forward moving than sentences using the passive voice.

However, sometimes we do not want to let our audience know who did the action, particularly if the soccer ball broke a window! For example, in the following sentence, "The soccer ball was kicked through the window," no one knows that Mary is the one who kicked the ball.

Carefully read the following sentences and mark "Yes" (Y) if the sentence uses the passive voice and "No" (N) if the sentence does not use the passive voice.

1. Tom was hurried to the hospital by his mother. _____

2. Caesar was murdered by his enemies. _____

3. Antirhodos was buried under the sea after more than 1,600 years ago by floods and earthquakes. _____

4. Cleopatra was forced from her throne. _____

5. Ptolemy forced Cleopatra from the throne. _____

6. Cleopatra was forced from her throne by Ptolemy. _____

7. Antirhodos was near Alexandria. _____

8. People are enchanted by Cleopatra's story. _____

9. Gaddio hopes to set up an underwater museum. _____

10. Visitors will explore Cleopatra's world close up. _____

Graphic Development

Directions: Read the information given below and use it and the hieroglyphics alphabet to translate the following message. Circle the correct translation.

Hieroglyphics are a form of picture writing used in ancient Egypt. These ancient writings and drawings helped locate the lost island Antirhodos. An alphabet of hieroglyphics is given below. In this alphabet, each picture represents a number or a letter in the English language. Note that one hieroglyph may represent more than one number or letter.

The hieroglyphics below are greatly simplified. The actual hieroglyphics of ancient Egypt are very complex and difficult to translate, and, of course, the language being written would be ancient Egyptian and not English.

The alphabet:

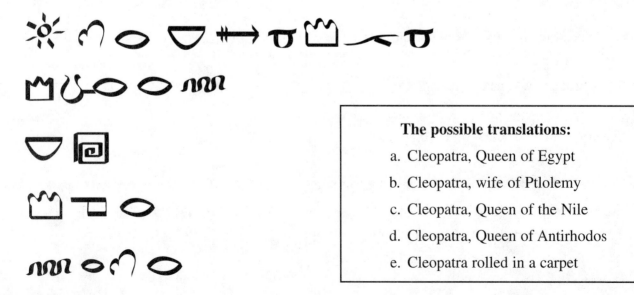

The message:

The possible translations:

a. Cleopatra, Queen of Egypt

b. Cleopatra, wife of Ptlolemy

c. Cleopatra, Queen of the Nile

d. Cleopatra, Queen of Antirhodos

e. Cleopatra rolled in a carpet

Sentence Comprehension

Directions: Read the sentence carefully and answer the following questions "True" (T) or "False" (F).

In a 1996 survey of 115 Ohio elementary schools with mediation programs, two out of three noted a decrease in fights, and more than half said fewer kids were being sent to the principal's office.

1. Every school in Ohio participated in the study. _____

2. Mediation programs in schools seem to promote misbehavior. _____

3. More than 50% of the Ohio schools with mediation programs showed an improvement in behavior. _____

4. Children are no longer sent to the principal's office if their school has a mediation program. _____

5. Mediation programs are a positive way to spend school money. _____

Word Study

Directions: Read the information given below and use it to answer the following questions "True" (T) or "False" (F).

Mediate

To *mediate* is a verb meaning to come between hostile or antagonistic people for the purpose of settling their difficulties. A *mediator*, a noun, is a person who mediates. *Mediation*, also a noun, is the act of *mediating*. *Mediated* is the adjective form of *to mediate*.

Mediate comes from the Latin *medius*, in the middle. Some highways have a *median*, a raised strip dividing one side of the road from the other so cars going in the opposite direction do not run into each other. In measurement, a *median* is a midpoint.

1. A mediator can be found on a major highway. _____

2. The midpoint on a ruler is the median. _____

3. The act of mediation tries to bring angry people to an agreement. _____

4. An agreement between two hostile persons could finally be mediated by the median. _____

5. A mediator can be helpful in settling an argument. _____

Paragraph Comprehension

Directions: Read the paragraph below and answer the following questions.

Many U.S. elementary schools are starting to give kids more responsibility for discipline. In the past 10 years, one-tenth of the nation's 86,000 public schools have started programs to resolve conflicts, mostly in middle or high schools. But educators want to begin more mediation programs sooner. They say elementary-age kids are even better at talking about their feelings and deciding on a fair solution than older kids are! When a teacher or principal is not involved, "kids talk more freely," says Glengarry Principal Loraine Johnson.

1. Mediation programs can begin

    a. in elementary school.

    b. in middle school.

    c. in high school.

    d. all of the above

2. The United States has approximately

    a. 86,000 reports of violence per year.

    b. 86,000 conflict resolution programs.

    c. 86,000 public schools.

    d. 86,000 teachers who are mediators.

3. According to the principal of Glengarry School, teachers are not part of mediation

    a. because they don't care.

    b. because they don't believe it is effective.

    c. so that the students can be open and honest.

    d. because they are not properly trained.

4. Which statement is false?

    a. Elementary-age children are capable of being involved in mediation programs.

    b. Students are involved in running the mediation programs.

    c. Conflict resolution programs are very different from mediation programs.

    d. Teachers feel mediation causes positive results.

5. What has happened to conflict resolution programs in the past 10 years?

    a. They have increased.

    b. They have decreased.

    c. They have stayed the same.

    d. The paragraph does not tell us.

Whole Story Comprehension

Directions: Read the story below and answer the questions on the following page.

Keep the Grownups Out of It

Sixth-grader Ivory Kelly finished up an English assignment at the blackboard. Then . . . Ping! Ping! He felt staples pelting his head. The 12-year-old knew just who was dissing him. He spun around and shouted at DeAngela Byrd. DeAngela claimed she was innocent. Then she called Ivory a "guinea pig." "Hosemouth!" he yelled back.

Their teacher, Linda Mann, didn't send them to the principal. She didn't even make them stand in the hall. Instead, she sent them to work things out in a small storage room in this Nashville, Tennessee, school. The room is Glengarry Elementary's mediation (me-dee-ay-shun) center.

Mediation in school is a way to solve disputes without having teachers punish students. Kids called mediators are trained to listen to classmates accused of misbehaving or fighting. Without taking sides, the mediators help troubled kids come up with their own solutions. It usually takes no more than 15 minutes.

At Glengarry, 30 students from third through sixth grade are trained to settle fights. After calmly discussing the staple attack and name calling with sixth-grade mediators, Michael Reese and Tracie Thacker, Ivory and DeAngela signed a pledge "not to mess with each other."

Many U.S. elementary schools are starting to give kids more responsibility for discipline. In the past 10 years, one-tenth of the nation's 86,000 public schools have staffed programs to resolve conflicts, mostly in middle or high schools. But educators want to begin more mediation programs sooner. They say elementary-age kids are even better at talking about their feelings and deciding on a fair solution than older kids are! When a teacher or principal is not involved, "kids talk more freely," says Glengarry Principal Loraine Johnson.

So far, mediation seems to work well. In a 1996 survey of 115 Ohio elementary schools with mediation programs, two out of three noted a decrease in fights, and more than half said fewer kids were being sent to the principal's office. In New Mexico, reports of bad behavior in elementary schools have dropped 85% since mediation programs began.

Glengarry mediator David Townlye, 11, says the method really works and not just in school. He used his new skills to help end a long-running battle between his grandmother and mother. "My grandmother thought my mother kept spending too much on flowers she planted outside our house," said David. "I let both of them talk. Finally, my mother agreed not to spend so much." Nobody had to stand in the corner either.

Whole Story Comprehension (cont.)

Directions: After you have read the story on the previous page, answer the questions below.

1. Conflict resolution and mediation are
   a. two programs that have the same goals.
   b. programs in which students work with their peers to solve disputes.
   c. a and b
   d. None of the above

2. Students trained in mediation
   a. are like lawyers; each mediator defends a student involved in the conflict.
   b. are neutral, never taking sides.
   c. provide a resolution for the students who are fighting.
   d. pick the punishment for the students who misbehaved.

3. Glengarry is the name of
   a. a principal.
   b. a school.
   c. a mediator.
   d. a town.

4. What do students do in a mediation center?
   a. They talk about the fight.
   b. They fight it out.
   c. They decide on a fair solution.
   d. a and c

5. Mediation can be considered a valuable life skill because
   a. you will always remember being a mediator in elementary school.
   b. it is a skill you can use in all areas of life.
   c. there are jobs for mediators.
   d. someday it may save your life.

6. Choose the correct word to fill in the blank. The _____ is trained to help classmates settle disputes.
   a. mediation
   b. mediated
   c. principal
   d. mediator

7. The 1996 survey of schools in Ohio that participated in mediation programs
   a. proves that mediation stops all school violence.
   b. reports that programs are not effective.
   c. shows participating schools have a decrease in bad behavior.
   d. shows that more teachers need to be mediators.

8. Successful conflict resolution between students depends on
   a. teacher and parent support.
   b. being willing to discuss conflicts openly and honestly.
   c. student volunteers.
   d. all of the above

Enrichment

Directions: Read the following information and use it to choose the best verb for the situations described below.

In the English language, there are many different verbs you can use to indicate how someone is speaking. You can find such words in the article you just read: *said, shout, diss, called, yelled.* Verbs to show someone who might be nervous while speaking are *mumble, stutter,* and *stammer.* Verbs to suggest someone is excited are *shout, yell,* or *scream.* Other verbs might be used to indicate someone might be unhappy: *whine, grumble, complain, weep, groan, moan,* or *sob.* If you were writing about someone who was trying to get another person to do something, you could use such verbs as *insist, argue, maintain,* or *urge.* Verbs to show someone might be trying to get other people to understand something are *explain, explicate,* or *interpret.* If you wanted to indicate that someone is not telling the truth, then you would use such verbs as *lie, fib, prevaricate,* or *equivocate.* There are even verbs to indicate that someone is trying to be funny: *joke, tease, quip,* and *wisecrack.*

1. The frightened boy began to speak in front of 500 people, "Good evening," he
   a) mumbled.
   b) grumbled.
   c) moaned.

2. "My mother forgot to give me my lunch money, and I had to go back home," she
   a) shouted.
   b) grumbled.
   c) stuttered.

3. She _____ with joy, "I've won the lottery!"
   a) screamed
   b) maintained
   c) whispered

4. "Take your vitamins. They are good for you," the doctor
   a) mumbled.
   b) urged.
   c) whined.

5. The thief _____, "But I don't know how it got in my pocket."
   a) explicated
   b) teased
   c) prevaricated

6. "*Hair* today, gone tomorrow," the comedian
   a) quipped.
   b) explained.
   c) sobbed.

7. "My cat died. I've lost my best friend," Aunt Sara
   a) sobbed.
   b) explained.
   c) argued.

8. "By the time I get through the cafeteria line, there is never any chocolate cake left," Harry
   a) complained.
   b) shouted.
   c) fibbed.

9. "Do your homework every night," the principal
   a) urged.
   b) explained.
   c) argued.

10. "I hate it when she _____. I can never understand what she is saying."
    a) yells
    b) fibs
    c) insists

Graphic Development

Directions: One way of classifying information is by placing it in categories. The three categories in the chart printed below are "cause," "effect," or "both cause and effect." If an action creates a reaction in someone or something else, then it is a cause. If an action is a result of someone else's behavior, then it is an effect. Some actions may be both. Read the statements written below and sort the statements according to the three categories.

Cause (C)	Effect (E)	Both Cause and Effect (CE)

1. Ivory feels staples hitting his head while he is at the blackboard.

2. Ivory and DeAngela sign a pledge.

3. Ms. Mann sends Ivory and DeAngela to the mediation center.

4. The mediators at the mediation center get Ivory and DeAngela to talk.

5. DeAngela claims she is innocent of throwing staples.

Sentence Comprehension

Directions: Read the sentence carefully and answer the following questions "True" (T) or "False" (F).

> At the museum's entrance, each bright, silky flag stands for a nation where, centuries ago, Africans were brought to be slaves.

1. The flags that line the museum's entrance represent the countries from which the Africans came. _____

2. Slavery is a part of African-American history. _____

3. The museum probably has an exhibit about slavery. _____

4. The museum opened centuries ago. _____

5. There is more than one flag at the entrance of the museum. _____

Word Study

Directions: Read the information given below and use it to answer the following questions "True" (T) or "False" (F).

> **Facet**
>
> *Facet* comes from the French word *facette*. It means a little face. *Face* used in this sense means a very small flat surface, like the face of a watch. But *facets* can be even smaller. A diamond sparkles because light is reflected from its many tiny *facets*. *Facet* can also be used to describe the many sides or aspects of a subject. For example, a teacher may explain the many *facets* of the Revolutionary War.
>
> *Facet* should not be confused with *faucet*, the plumbing fixture found in a kitchen sink or a bathroom. A *faucet* is used to take water from a pipe. A *faucet* could also be attached to a container such as a barrel so that someone could draw a liquid from it.

1. A diamond has *facets*. _____

2. The study of the science has many *facets*. _____

3. *Facet* was a word first used in the Revolutionary War. _____

4. A *faucet* may be found only on a kitchen or bathroom sink. _____

5. *Faucet* and *facet* mean the same thing. _____

Paragraph Comprehension

Directions: Read the paragraph below and answer the following questions.

Detroit was one of the last stops on the Underground Railroad for slaves escaping to the promised land of Canada. Many African Americans migrated to Detroit from the 1920s through the l950s to work in automobile and defense factories. The defense factories made guns and other supplies needed by the armed forces to fight in World War II. Today, Detroit's 750,000 African Americans are proud that their city is home to the new museum. Organ says, "It makes sense to have it here."

1. The Underground Railroad is

   a. a subway.

   b. a defense factory.

   c. an escape route north for slaves.

   d. a train factory.

2. From the 1920s to the 1950s

   a. African-American slaves escaped to Canada.

   b. Detroit's population was 750,000.

   c. a new museum was built in Detroit.

   d. work opportunities in Detroit encouraged many African Americans to move there.

3. In the paragraph, the "promised land" refers to

   a. Detroit.

   b. Canada.

   c. employment opportunities.

   d. factories.

4. Where is the new museum located?

   a. Detroit

   b. Africa

   c. Canada

   d. underground

5. What does "migrated to Detroit" mean?

   a. There was only work in the summer.

   b. It is another way to say African-American people flew there.

   c. African Americans walked to Detroit.

   d. African Americans relocated to Detroit.

Whole Story Comprehension

Directions: Read the story below and answer the questions on the following page.

Remembering Their Journey

When Frederick and Katrina Jones visit the Museum of African-American History in Detroit, Michigan, they can see the great achievements of black Americans from past generations. They can also see themselves. Katrina, 13, and her brother Frederick, 11, are part of a museum exhibit. Molds of their faces and bodies were used to make statues of Africans, shown on a model slave ship.

"Vaseline covered my body before paper-mâché was applied from my stomach to my feet and later my face and upper body," Katrina recalls. "I couldn't move for over an hour, and I couldn't talk, because moving or talking would have cracked the mold."

"Seeing myself is kind of fun," says Frederick. "It was nice that kids got to do something about our heritage." When he grows up, Frederick hopes he can show his family the youthful model and say, "That's me!"

The museum, created in 1965, moved into a grand new home in April, 1997. It is now the largest African American history museum anywhere. People talk about African Americans during Black History Month, but this museum celebrates the achievements of black Americans year-round.

"The purpose of the museum is to preserve the history and culture of African Americans," says Rita Organ, curator of the museum. "I hope people will see that the contributions African Americans make extend into every facet of life and play an important part in American culture."

Visitors are greeted by a splash of bright, silky flags at the museum's entrance. Each flag stands for a nation, where centuries ago, Africans were brought to be slaves.

In the museum's Ring of Fame, the names of 60 great Africans and African Americans grace the floor. Visitors to the inventor's area can see George Grant's invention, the golf tee. Also on display is Samella Lewis' original drawing for the design on the dime and the first traffic signal, invented by Garrett Morgan. The Congressional Medal of Honor awarded to Christian Fleetwood is among Organ's favorite items on display. Sergeant Major Fleetwood earned it for heroism in a Civil War battle.

Detroit was one of the last stops on the Underground Railroad for slaves escaping to the "promised land" of Canada. Many African Americans migrated to Detroit from the 1920s through the 1950s to work in automobile and defense factories. The defense factories made guns and other supplies needed by the armed forces to fight in World War II. Today Detroit's 750,000 African Americans are proud that their city is home to the new museum. Organ says, "It makes sense to have it here."

Whole Story Comprehension *(cont.)*

Directions: After you have read the story on the previous page, answer the questions below.

1. Katrina and Fredrick are in the Museum of African-American History because

   a. they are very famous.

   b. they were models for the statues in an exhibit.

   c. they work there.

   d. they invented molds.

2. Rita Organ

   a. owns the museum.

   b. visited the museum last year.

   c. cares for the museum and its exhibits.

   d. is honored in the museum.

3. Katrina and Frederick became models for the statues of Africans because

   a. it was an easy way to make money.

   b. their parents told them to.

   c. it was an honor to represent their ancestors.

   d. they wanted all of their friends to see them.

4. The exhibit that names 60 great African Americans is called the

   a. Medal of Honor.

   b. Promised Land.

   c. Ring of Fame.

   d. Museum of African-American History.

5. Black History Month

   a. honors the achievements of African Americans.

   b. celebrates African-American culture.

   c. preserves African-American heritage.

   d. all of the above

6. The curator of the museum believes Detroit is an appropriate site for the museum because

   a. the Underground Railroad makes it easy to get to.

   b. of the large African-American population in that city.

   c. it is open year-round.

   d. of Detroit's significance in African-American history.

7. Christian Fleetwood is honored in the museum for

   a. receiving the Congressional Medal of Honor.

   b. being a hero.

   c. a and b

   d. being a sergeant in the Civil War.

8. Some items seen in the museum are

   a. a sketch of the dime's design.

   b. the first traffic light.

   c. the first golf tee.

   d. all of the above

Enrichment

Directions: Read the information in the box below and use it to determine which method is used in each sentence. Write the letter that corresponds to the correct method for each sentence.

The sentences in the article you have just read do not always start the same way.

 a. The usual way we *start a sentence is with a subject and its modifiers.* Here are three sentences that start the usual way. "The museum moved into a grand new home." "Detroit was one of the last stops." "The defense factories made guns."

But it is possible to vary the way we begin sentences so that the reader does not get bored with our writing style.

 b. We can *place the subject after the verb.* "Also on display is Samella Lewis' original drawing." "Here is the new museum."

 c. Or we can *begin a sentence with a dependent clause*: "When Frederick and Katrina Jones visit the museum, they can see themselves." "When he grows up, Frederick hopes to show his family."

 d. Or another way we can *begin a sentence is with a prepositional phrase.* "In the museum's Ring of Fame, the names of 60 great Americans grace the floor."

 e. Or we can *begin with an adjective or adverb.* "Today, Detroit's 750,000 African Americans are proud." "Created by Garrett Morgan, the traffic signal was an important invention."

 f. Or we can *begin with an infinitive.* "To honor African Americans, the Ring of Fame was created."

_____ 1. Aware of the problems, they nevertheless decided to continue.

_____ 2. While my friends were waiting for the movie to begin, they ate two tubs of popcorn.

_____ 3. With great joy, we watched our team win.

_____ 4. At the end of my block, a deserted building stands.

_____ 5. To prove his point, he turned to the encyclopedia.

_____ 6. Forced to stay after school, they refused to do their homework.

_____ 7. I am lost in a large city.

_____ 8. The large brown dog was growling at me.

_____ 9. Here comes the rain.

_____ 10. There were hundreds of people at the concert.

Graphic Development

Directions: Use the clues to fill in the numbered blanks on the time line. Choose your answers from the box below.

Time Line of Inventions by African Americans and Other Events

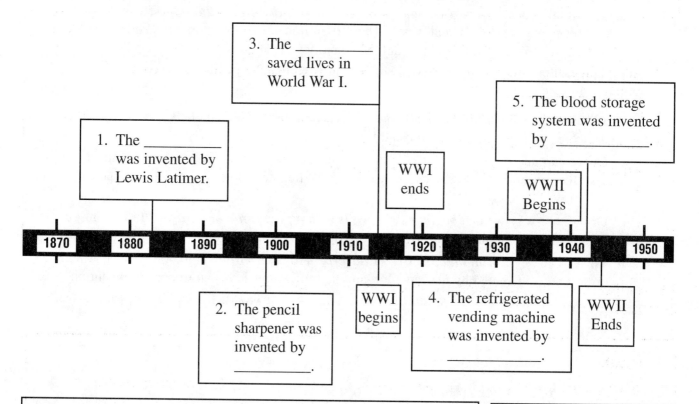

Clues:

The carbon filament for the light bulb was invented before the pencil sharpener.

Charles Drew's invention was created during World War II.

Sandy Love did not invent the pencil sharpener or the blood storage system.

J. J. Love's invention was created before that of Sandy Love.

Golf was popular during the 20th century.

Garrett Morgan's invention saved many lives because it was used in World War I.

Charles Drew invented the system for storing blood for emergency use.

George Grant invented the golf tee.

Samella Lewis invented the design on the dime.

Sandy Love invented the refrigerated vending machine.

J. J. Love invented the pencil sharpener.

Garrett Morgan invented the traffic signal.

Possible Answers

a. carbon filament for the light bulb
b. Charles Drew
c. J. J. Love
d. Sandy Love
e. gas mask

Sentence Comprehension

Directions: Read the sentence carefully and answer the following questions "True" (T) or "False" (F).

> A huge rush in South Africa, once the diamond capital of the world, was sparked by a 15-year-old's lucky diamond find in a bed of gravel.

1. A 15-year-old found a diamond during the diamond rush in South Africa. _____

2. At one time, more diamonds were found in South Africa than anywhere else in the world. _____

3. Diamonds can only be found in mines. _____

4. South Africa is the diamond capital of the world. _____

5. After the diamond was found, many others came to South Africa hoping to find diamonds. _____

Word Study

Directions: Read the information given below and use it to answer the following questions "True" (T) or "False" (F).

> **Mantle**
>
> In the article, we learn that most diamonds "were formed billions of years ago in an inner layer of the earth called the *mantle*." Geologists, people who study the earth, tell us that the earth is like a ball with three layers. A *mantle*, or *mantlerock*, covers the central core. The lithosphere, or outer covering, made up mostly of rock, lies on top of the mantle.
>
> Geologists named this middle layer a *mantle* because the word means to cover as if with a *mantle*. This word has been in the English language since the 12th century when men and women wore *mantles*, or very long loose sleeveless coats, over their clothing, like long vests.
>
> The lantern we use when we go camping uses a *mantle*. In this case, it is a lacy hood that is placed over the flame to cause it to give extra light.
>
> The *mantel* over a fireplace serves as support rather than a covering and is not spelled the same way.

1. A *mantle* is the same as a *mantel*. _____

2. The word *mantle* has been in the English language for a long time. _____

3. A *mantle* makes a flame brighter in a camping lantern. _____

4. The outer layer of the earth is called a *mantle*. _____

5. Geologists are able to tell us how the earth is composed. _____

Paragraph Comprehension

Directions: Read the information given below and answer the following questions "True" (T) or "False" (F).

Most diamonds were formed billions of years ago in an inner layer of the earth called the mantle. About 100 miles underground, the mantle puts extreme heat (1,800 degrees Fahrenheit) and pressure on carbon, the common black substance in coal and pencils. These forces turn black carbon into clear diamond crystal. As the crystal grows, it may trap other chemicals inside, creating what Harlow calls "a space capsule from the inner earth."

1. A diamond is formed from

    a. carbon and heat.

    b. coal and heat.

    c. carbon, heat, and pressure.

    d. black crystals and chemicals.

2. The mantle

    a. was formed millions of years ago.

    b. created a lot of heat and pressure underground.

    c. is a layer of black carbon.

    d. was created by heat and pressure.

3. The earth's mantle

    a. is always 1,800 degrees Fahrenheit.

    b. is the place where coal is formed.

    c. is the layer of the earth in which diamonds are mined.

    d. traps chemicals to form crystals.

4. What is the basic element that forms a diamond?

    a. carbon

    b. coal

    c. chemicals

    d. crystals

5. Clear diamond crystals

    a. were formed millions or even billions of years ago.

    b. are used in pencils.

    c. are formed 1,800 miles under the earth's surface.

    d. are used to make space capsules.

Enrichment

Directions: Read the information below and use it to match the correct items.

Idioms

Diamonds are not only found in the ground, in industry, and in jewelry, they can also be found in idioms. An *idiom* occurs when a new meaning is given to a group of words that already have their own meaning.

For example, a rough diamond is a diamond that has not been cut and polished. The finishing of the diamond makes it more beautiful and more valuable. But if we say, "Harry is a diamond in the rough," we do not mean that Harry is an actual, unfinished diamond. What we mean is that Harry is a good person who seems rough or impolite. With training or experience, he could become better. When we say that John looks awkward for a ball player, but he is a rough diamond, we mean that with training and practice, John has the ability to become a very good ball player.

There are a number of idioms that can be used to describe people. Some are positive: "She has a heart of gold." "He is a good egg." Some are negative: "He is as hard as nails." "He is a cold fish." "He's a pain in the neck."

Some idioms describe how an individual relates to others. "Her ideas are off the wall." "He is a bit of an oddball." "He has gone off his rocker." All these idioms describe people who are strange.

Match the idioms with the descriptions of individuals in a classroom.

Descriptions

1. someone who learns something every easily
2. the person who always compliments the teacher
3. someone who can't keep a secret
4. the one who gets the best grades
5. a person who is always late

Idioms

a. an apple polisher
b. the head of the class
c. a slowpoke
d. a quick study
e. a big mouth

Here is another set that relates to praise and criticism. Match the idiom with the description of a person or a thing.

6. a person who can make plants grow
7. a very delicious piece of chocolate cake
8. a person who is easily frightened
9. a person who cannot be trusted
10. a person who wants something for nothing

f. a snake in the grass
g. to have one's cake and eat it too
h. out of this world
i. one who has a green thumb
j. a chicken

Graphic Development

Directions: Look carefully at the map and match the continents with their products. Write the letter that corresponds to the correct continent for each product.

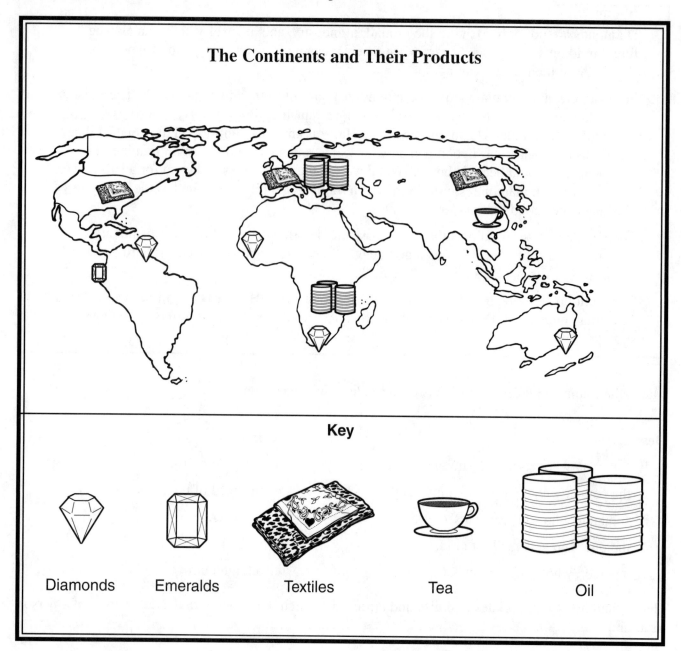

The Continents and Their Products

Key

Diamonds   Emeralds   Textiles   Tea   Oil

The products

1. diamond and emeralds _____
2. textiles and tea _____
3. only textiles _____
4. only diamonds _____
5. diamonds and oil _____
6. textiles and oil _____

The continents

a. Africa
b. Europe
c. Asia
d. Australia
e. South America
f. North America

Sentence Comprehension

Directions: Read the sentence carefully and answer the following questions "True" (T) or "False" (F).

> A study by Dr. Charlotte Alexander of Houston, Texas, showed that, on average, kids carry a backpack that weighs 10% of what they weigh.

1. The study in Houston, Texas, involved school children. _____

2. Dr. Alexander studies overweight children. _____

3. *On average* means most. _____

4. When someone conducts a study, he or she gathers information about a topic. _____

5. You must be a doctor to conduct a study. _____

Word Study

Directions: Read the information given below and use it to answer the following questions "True" (T) or "False" (F).

> An *orthopedic* surgeon is a doctor who specializes in preventing or correcting physical problems in the human skeleton. *Ortho-* means straight or upright. We visit an *orthodontist* who gives us braces and other devices to correct our crooked teeth. Some religious groups are more *orthodox* than others. They practice their religious beliefs in what they see as the correct or right way. Thus, we see *ortho-* in the terms *Orthodox* Jews or the Greek *Orthodox* Church.
>
> The second part of the word *orthopedic* is *-pedic*. *Pedic* relates to child. *Pediatrics* is a branch of medicine dealing with children's care and diseases. A *pediatrician* specializes in children's medicine, but an *orthopedist* may treat adults as well.
>
> But if someone has problems with his or her bones, then it would be wise to see an *orthopedist* before the person is fully-grown. An *orthopedist* may also prescribe braces to help correct a deformity.

1. Only orthodontists prescribe braces to correct deformities. _____

2. A pediatrician treats only children. _____

3. An orthopedist tries to prevent physical problems. _____

4. Orthodox means the correct way. _____

5. An orthopedist treats only adults. _____

Paragraph Comprehension

Directions: Read the information given below and answer the following questions.

Jordan isn't the only one who needs to lighten his load. In October, 1999, the American Academy of Orthopedic Surgeons (A.A.O.S.) reported that thousands of kids have back, neck, and shoulder pain caused by their heavy backpacks. The A.A.O.S. surveyed more than 100 physicians in Illinois and Delaware. More than half said they have treated kids for pain and muscle fatigue caused by backpacks. The Consumer Product Safety Commission found that in 1998, U.S. kids ages five to 14 made 10,062 visits to doctors' offices with backpack-caused aches.

1. The American Academy of Orthopedic Surgeons conducted a survey in

   a. the U.S.

   b. Jordan.

   c. Illinois and Delaware.

   d. a doctor's office.

2. What is the cause of school age children's back pain?

   a. poorly constructed backpacks

   b. overloaded backpacks

   c. too much homework

   d. muscle aches

3. *Lighten his load* means

   a. to pack his backpack better.

   b. to lose weight.

   c. to worry less.

   d. to carry less in a backpack.

4. What is the least number of physicians from Illinois and Delaware who said they have treated children for pain and muscle fatigue?

   a. 49

   b. 50

   c. 51

   d. 20

5. Why did 10,062 U.S. students need medical attention in 1998?

   a. to participate in the A.A.O.S. study

   b. to get help with tired muscles and back pain

   c. to help reduce the weight they carry

   d. to follow the recommendations of the Consumer Product Safety Commission

Whole Story Comprehension

Directions: Read the story below and answer the questions on the following page.

A Real Pain in the Neck

Carrying a backpack can be hazardous to your health. Just ask Jordan Morgan, 10, of California. "One time I fell off my bike and bruised my leg because my backpack was too heavy," says Jordan. He weighs 100 pounds. His backpack, loaded with four books, a calculator, a binder, paper, glue, and gym clothes, can weigh 20 pounds! "Sometimes I have to stop and rest because it's too heavy."

Jordan isn't the only one who needs to lighten his load. In October, 1999, the American Academy of Orthopedic Surgeons (A.A.O.S.) reported that thousands of kids have back, neck, and shoulder pain caused by their heavy backpacks. The A.A.O.S. surveyed more than 100 physicians in Illinois and Delaware. More than half said they have treated kids for pain and muscle fatigue caused by backpacks. The Consumer Product Safety Commission found that in 1998, U.S. kids ages five to 14 made 10,062 visits to doctors' offices with backpack-caused aches.

Half the doctors in the A.A.O.S. survey said a backpack can do some damage if it weighs 20 pounds or more. A study by Dr. Charlotte Alexander of Houston, Texas, showed that, on average, kids carry a backpack that weighs 10 percent of what they weigh. "That's not a problem," says Dr. Alexander, "but we found one 10 year-old with a backpack weighing 47 pounds!"

How should you carry a heavy load? Use both shoulder straps, place the heaviest items closest to your back, and bend both knees when lifting. If you have lots to carry, try a backpack with hip straps or wheels.

Jordan Morgan is packing lighter now and feeling better. Says Jordan, "I don't fall anymore or hurt myself."

Whole Story Comprehension (cont.)

Directions: After you have read the story on the previous page, answer the questions below.

1. How much heavier than average is Jordan's backpack?

   a. 10 pounds
   b. 20 pounds
   c. 100 pounds
   d. more than 20 pounds

2. What probably caused Jordan to fall off his bike?

   a. a bruised leg
   b. muscle fatigue
   c. lack of balance because of a heavy backpack
   d. being 20% overweight

3. What is the proper way to distribute the weight of your backpack?

   a. Find a 10-year-old to carry it.
   b. Use two shoulder straps and place the heavier items closest to your back.
   c. Use two shoulder straps and place the lighter items closest to your back.
   d. Carry the backpack across your hips.

4. The American Academy of Orthopedic Surgeons chose to study this medical problem

   a. to save the insurance companies money.
   b. because more children were going to the doctor with back and neck pain, and they wanted to know the cause.
   c. because the Consumer Product Safety Commission wants to redesign backpacks.
   d. because schools wanted to ban backpacks as a health hazard.

5. A safe weight for a backpack is

   a. more than 20 pounds.
   b. 10% of your body weight.
   c. 47 pounds for a student 10 years old or older.
   d. unknown.

6. Who initiated the heavy-backpack study?

   a. Consumer Product Safety Commission
   b. American Academy of Orthopedic Surgeons
   c. Dr. Charlotte Alexander
   d. Jordan Morgan

7. If you have a very heavy load to carry, what should you do?

   a. Ask for less homework.
   b. Use a carryall with wheels.
   c. See a doctor afterwards.
   d. Buy a heavy-duty backpack.

8. To prevent back injury, you can

   a. weigh your backpack, calculate the maximum weight, and carry only what you need.
   b. switch the sides on which you carry your backpack.
   c. never bring books home.
   d. a and b

Enrichment

Directions: Read the information below and use it to match the problem with the doctor who specializes in treatment for that particular problem.

In addition to orthopedists, orthodontists, and pediatricians, there are a number of doctors who specialize in various branches of medicine. Except for *doctor*, *physician*, *obstetrician*, *surgeon*, and *pediatrician*, most names of these medical specialists end with "-ist."

A word ending in "-ist" signals that the word relates to someone who performs a specific action or specializes in a specific field. A cyclist is one who rides a bicycle. A chemist is one who studies chemistry. An internist specializes in internal medicine.

In medicine, there are many other specialists whose names end in "-ist."

- If we have a skin problem, we consult a *dermatologist*.
- If we have a heart problem, we consult a *cardiologist*.
- If we are allergic to various substances, we see an *allergist*.
- If we have a foot problem, we see a *podiatrist*.
- If we have mental problems, we see a *psychiatrist*.
- If we have an eye problem, we see an *ophthalmologist* or *optometrist*.
- If we have problems digesting, we see a *gastroenterologist*.

The problems

1. having a painful ingrown toenail
2. having blurry vision
3. having a skin rash that won't go away
4. sneezing constantly in the spring
5. having bad dreams every night
6. having a bad stomachache every time one eats
7. having a heart attack

The specialists

a. allergist
b. cardiologist
c. dermatologist
d. gastroentrologist
e. ophthalmologist or optometrist
f. podiatrist
g. psychiatrist

Graphic Development

Directions: Read the information below and use it to fill in the chart.

We learned from the article that the maximum weight for a backpack is 20% of an individual's weight. Dividing a number by 5 is the easiest way to find 20% of that number.

Harry is a sixth grader who weighs 125 pounds. If 125 is divided by 5, we discover that the weight of any backpack Harry carries should be no more than 25 pounds.

The chart lists five of Harry's classmates and their weights. Fill in the third column of the chart by choosing an answer from the lettered list of possible backpack weights.

Lettered List of Possible Backpack Weights

a. 24	g. 20
b. 23	h. 19
c. 22	i. 18
d. 23	j. 17
e. 25	k. 16
f. 21	l. 15

Students	Weight	Maximum weight of a backpack
Harry	125	*25*
Zack	90	1.
Keisha	85	2.
Jose	110	3.
Maria	105	4.
Amy	95	5.

Sentence Comprehension

Directions: Read the sentence carefully and answer the following questions "True" (T) or "False" (F).

> The murder of Jews by members of German's Nazi Party from 1938 to 1945 is known as the Holocaust.

1. The Nazi Party killed Jews. _____
2. The Holocaust was happening in 1942. _____
3. The Holocaust is a historical happening. _____
4. The Holocaust lasted a total of 5 years. _____
5. The Nazi Party was in Germany. _____

Word Study

Directions: Read the information given below and use it to answer the following questions "True" (T) or "False" (F).

> When we see the word *Holocaust*, with a capital letter, we think of the murder of Jews by the Nazis in World War II. This action was called a *holocaust* because the word without a capital letter means a thorough destruction. But the destruction usually takes place through fire or as sacrifice consumed by fire. We could say that a very bad fire was a *holocaust* if it caused huge losses.
>
> The Nazi destruction of the Jews is also sometimes called *genocide*. This is a systematic and deliberate destruction of a group of people. The group may be racial, political, or cultural.
>
> *Genocide* is made up of two parts, *geno-* and *-cide*. *Geno-* refers to race or type and *-cide* means killer, as in *insecticide* or *pesticide*. Many words end with *-cide*. *Homicide* is the killing of a human. *Infanticide* is the killing of a baby. None of these actions is approved by our society, including *suicide*, which is the killing of oneself.

1. *Genocide* and *holocaust* (without a capital) mean the same. _____
2. *Genocide* and *Holocaust* (with a capital) mean the same. _____
3. *Homicide* is the killing of a person. _____
4. A very bad forest fire in which thousands of trees were destroyed could be called a *holocaust*.
   _____
5. A systematic attack on a group of people in order to wipe them out completely is *genocide*.
   _____

Paragraph Comprehension

Directions: Read the paragraph below and answer the following questions.

Of the six million Jewish people who died in the Holocaust, 1.2 million were children. Eleanor Schiller, a teacher in Myrtle Beach, South Carolina, was looking for a way to help her students understand the huge number of young lives lost in the Holocaust. After she read Friedmann's poem, an idea took flight. She decided to invite students everywhere to create 1,200,000 paper butterflies to display for Holocaust Remembrance Day on April 23, 1998. Says Schiller: "I wanted kids to realize that this is a world where we can all work together."

1. Eleanor Schiller wanted her students to create 1,200,000 butterflies

    a. to decorate for Remembrance Day.

    b. because a poem written by Pavel gave her the idea.

    c. because butterflies all live together peacefully.

    d. to give her students a better understanding of how many lives were lost.

2. Which subject was Ms. Schiller's class most likely studying when they took on the butterfly project?

    a. science

    b. math

    c. social studies

    d. literature

3. Ms. Schiller's class planned to

    a. complete the butterfly project alone.

    b. visit on Holocaust Remembrance Day.

    c. ask other school children to help them reach their goal.

    d. learn about the Holocaust.

4. About how many Jewish people died in the Holocaust?

    a. 7.2 million adults and children

    b. 6 million

    c. 1,200,000

    d. 1.2 million

5. What inspired Ms. Schiller to create the 1,200,000 butterflies?

    a. Pavel Friedmann's poem "The Butterfly"

    b. a book she read about the Holocaust

    c. her students' inability to understand the concept of one million

    d. a visit to the Holocaust memorial

Whole Story Comprehension

Directions: Read the story below and answer the questions on the following page.

A Million Butterflies

When Pavel Friedmann was about 11 years old, his family was forced to leave their home in Poland. The Friedmanns and other Jewish families were moved into a walled-off, isolated area called a ghetto. While he was living in the ghetto, Pavel wrote a poem called "The Butterfly." Part of the poem reads: "Such a yellow / Is carried lightly way up high / It went away I'm sure because it wished to kiss the world goodbye."

It was the last butterfly Pavel would ever see. He was one of six million Jewish people who were killed during World War II. The murder of Jews by members of German's Nazi Party from 1938 to 1945 is known as the Holocaust. It is considered to be one of the most evil acts in history.

Of the six million Jewish people who died in the Holocaust, 1.2 million were children. Eleanor Schiller, a teacher in Myrtle Beach, South Carolina, was looking for a way to help her students understand the huge number of young lives lost in the Holocaust. After she read Friedmann's poem, an idea took flight. She decided to invite students everywhere to create 1,200,000 paper butterflies to display for Holocaust Remembrance Day on April 23, 1998. Says Schiller: "I wanted kids to realize that this is a world where we can all work together."

The students at Schiller's religious school, Chabad Academy, cut out butterflies for weeks. By March, they had made about 125,000 butterflies.

Student Becky Hemmo, 13, says the project was special to her. "Butterflies are just like children—colorful and free. Butterflies don't live long, and these kids didn't live long. We should remember what happened to stop it from ever happening again."

Whole Story Comprehension *(cont.)*

Directions: After you have read the story on the previous page, answer the questions below.

1. What was the name of a separated section of a city where Jewish people were required to live during World War II?

   a. ghetto

   b. Germany

   c. Myrtle Beach

   d. academy

2. Which of the following statements is not true?

   a. Pavel Friedmann was a victim of the Holocaust.

   b. Pavel Friedmann's homeland was Germany.

   c. Pavel Friedmann's poem inspired the paper butterfly project.

   d. The butterflies the students made are like the children murdered in the Holocaust.

3. Where does the butterfly in Pavel's poem go?

   a. It dies.

   b. It is captured.

   c. It flies away.

   d. It goes back home.

4. Of what was Pavel dreaming when he wrote "The Butterfly"?

   a. freedom

   b. escape

   c. a better life

   d. all of the above

5. The paper butterflies were supposed to represent

   a. the children who learned about the Holocaust.

   b. the children the Nazis killed.

   c. all of the Holocaust victims.

   d. freedom.

6. If the students had created 125,000 butterflies by March, why is it likely that they would not reach their goal by April?

   a. 1.2 million is nearly ten times what they had created.

   b. The students were not interested.

   c. They ran out of paper.

   d. Holocaust Remembrance Day was canceled.

7. Holocaust Remembrance Day is a

   a. memorial.

   b. celebration.

   c. town in South Carolina.

   d. day you get off from school.

8. Which particular student had a positive experience with the butterfly project?

   a. Pavel Freedman

   b. Eleanor Scholar

   c. Becky Hemmo

   d. Myrtle Beach

Enrichment

Directions: Read the information below and use it to answer the following questions.

In the article, a short poem, "The Butterfly," is quoted. Part of the poem reads: "Such a yellow / Is carried lightly way up high / It went away I'm sure because it wished to kiss the world goodbye." There are certain rules of punctuation that are followed when we include poems in our writing.

First, the title of a short poem is placed in quotations. How short does a poem have to be? It has to be short enough to be included in a larger book. If the poem is so long that it is published in a book all by itself, the title is underlined or italicized.

Second, all the major words of the title, including the first word, are capitalized.

Third, the first line of each poem is capitalized, unless the poet did not use capitals e. e. cummings never used capitals in his poems nor in his name!

Fourth, if the whole poem, or four lines or more, are copied in a piece of writing, then all the lines are indented to set the poem off from the rest of the text. If a line or several lines of poetry need to be omitted, then the omitted material is placed with a line of dots the width of the poem.

Fifth, if only several lines are quoted, they can be introduced into a piece of writing with a colon, just as it was used in the article.

Sixth, a slash (/) is used to separate the lines of poetry that are not set off from the piece of writing. A space goes before and after the slash.

As you can see, poetry gets very special treatment.

Here is a short poem that a student quoted and then wrote about. (The poet is not e.e. cummings.) Mark "Yes" (Y) if each line is correctly written according to the six rules written above. Mark "No" (N) if it is not.

Poem	Lines
Dreams (title)	1.
Hold fast to dreams	2.
For if dreams die	3.
Life is a broken-winged bird	4.
That cannot fly	5.

Graphic Development

Directions: The graph below shows only a fraction of the 55 million lives lost in World War II. Interpret the data to fill in the blanks with the best answer choice from the list.

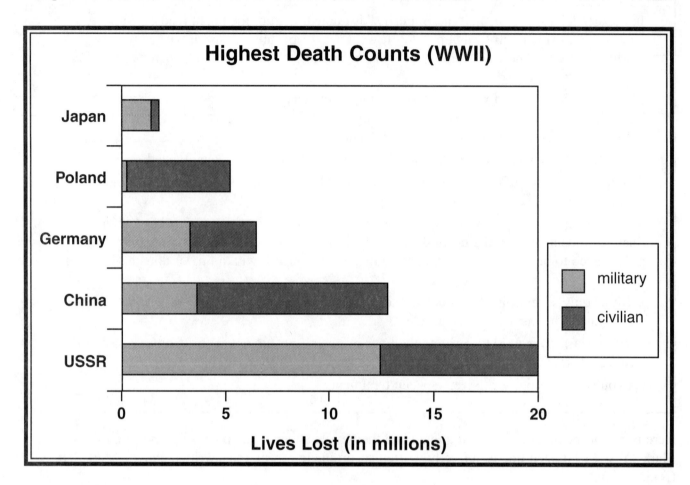

Highest Death Counts (WWII)

Lives Lost (in millions)

military
civilian

1. _____ suffered a total loss of about 13,500,000 lives.

2. _____ combined had more civilian deaths than military deaths.

3. _____ had civilian and military losses that were almost equal.

4. _____ China, and the USSR were all invaded by Germany. They had a combined civilian loss of 21,000,000.

5. _____ had a staggering military death count of approximately 13,000,000.

Possible answers:

    a. China

    b. Germany

    c. Poland and China

    d. Poland

    e. Germany and Japan

    f. USSR

Sentence Comprehension

Directions: Read the sentence carefully and answer the following questions "True" (T) or "False" (F).

> "Far and away the greatest threat to the ocean, and thus to ourselves, is ignorance," she says.

1. Education is an important step in protecting the ocean. _____

2. The ocean is necessary for sustaining life on earth. _____

3. *Far and away* means that only the most distant oceans are threatened. _____

4. The person speaking believes many people don't know enough about the ocean. _____

5. At this point, it is impossible to save the oceans. _____

Word Study

Directions: Read the information given below and use it to answer the following questions "True" (T) or "False" (F).

Astro- and **Aqua-**

Because of explorations in outer space, we are familiar with the word *astronaut*. An astronaut is a navigator in space beyond the earth's atmosphere. The first part of the word is *astro*. *Astro* relates to the stars or heavens. The second part of the word, *naut* relates to nautical. The Latin word for sailor is *nauticus*. Thus, an astronaut is like a sailor in the sky.

A less familiar word is *aquanaut*. The first part of the word is *aqua*. *Aqua* is the Latin word for water. An *aqueduct* is a long tunnel or trough on land by which large quantities of flowing water is moved. *Aquarius* is a constellation in the heavens that shows a man pouring water. An *aquanaut* is a scuba driver who lives and operates both inside and outside of an underwater shelter for an extended period of time. But another way of thinking of an aquanaut is as a sailor in the ocean.

---

1. *Aquanauts* are the same as sailors on the ocean. _____

2. *Astronauts* are similar to sailors in the sky. _____

3. Anything described as *nautical* has to do with only lakes. _____

4. *Aquanauts* use aqueducts to move from place to place in the ocean. _____

5. *Aquarius* is the name given to a group of stars that suggest a picture. _____

Paragraph Comprehension

Directions: Read the paragraph below and use it to answer the following questions.

Another threat comes from man-made fertilizers. They wash off fields into streams and eventually into the ocean. This encourages the harmful overgrowth of algae and the spread of toxic germs that can kill fish and cause human health problems. Billions of fish died along the middle and southern Atlantic coast of the U.S. in recent years. Pollution is the main suspect.

---

1. Fertilizers

   a. are often dumped directly into the ocean.

   b. help the ocean because fish eat algae.

   c. make algae grow and bacteria multiply.

   d. are used to kill fish.

2. In this paragraph, pollution is suspected of causing

   a. fish to be killed on the U.S. Atlantic coast.

   b. widespread human illness caused by toxic germs.

   c. fertilizers to wash off fields.

   d. toxic drinking water.

3. Algae overgrowth causes

   a. the spread of toxic germs.

   b. fish to die.

   c. human health problems.

   d. all of the above

4. How do the fertilizers get into the ocean?

   a. Rain washes them off fields into streams that run into the ocean.

   b. The people of the southern Atlantic coast are the main suspects.

   c. Local farmers wade in the ocean with dirty boots.

   d. Fishing boats dump them into the ocean.

5. How does ocean pollution affect human health?

   a. People will feel nauseous from the smell of dead fish.

   b. Fish will carry germs and diseases to the people who eat them.

   c. When the beaches close, people won't lie in the sun and get skin cancer.

   d. People will not be able to exercise by swimming because the ocean is polluted.

Whole Story Comprehension

Directions: Read the story below and use it to answer the questions on the following page.

Exploring the Deep

"You have to love it before you are moved to save it," says world-famous marine biologist Sylvia Earle. She is talking about the greatest love of her life, the ocean. If anyone in the world knows what it will take to save the millions of species that live in our oceans, it's Earle.

The oceans define the earth. They cover almost 75% of the planet and hold 97% of its water. Nearly half of the world's population lives within 60 miles of the sea. Scientists say that 10 million to 30 million species of sea life may still be undiscovered.

Earle, 63, takes fish personally. She has gone on at least 50 diving expeditions and spent more than 6,000 hours under the sea. In 1970, she was captain of the first team of women to live beneath the ocean's surface. The five "aquanauts" spent two weeks in a small underwater laboratory, a small structure off the U.S. Virgin Islands.

Since 1979, when she walked freely on the ocean floor 1,250 feet beneath the water's surface, Earle has been known as "Her Deepness." She holds the world's record for the deepest dive by any human outside of a submarine.

Now Earle has a new job: explorer-in-residence for the National Geographic Society. As the leader of a five-year project, Earle will use a zippy new submarine to study the waters of the 12 national marine sanctuaries. These are underwater areas similar to national parks that are protected by the U.S. government.

Earle is terribly concerned that people are polluting and over-using the ocean. Fishing methods that use trawlers to dredge the ocean floor also destroy underwater habitats. Earle calls the trawlers "bulldozers."

Another threat comes from man-made fertilizers. They wash off fields into streams and eventually into the ocean. This encourages the harmful overgrowth of algae and the spread of toxic germs that can kill fish and cause human health problems. Billions of fish have died along the middle and southern Atlantic coast of the U.S. in recent years. Pollution is the main suspect.

Earle offers several solutions to these problems. She urges people to take action to volunteer to clean a beach. She also hopes people will learn as much as they can about how the ocean keeps all of us alive. "Far and away the greatest threat to the ocean, and thus to ourselves, is ignorance," she says, "but we can do something about that."

Earle sits on a rock and stares out at her beloved sea. She claims the key to the earth's future is not to be found among the stars. "The future is here," she says, "on this aquatic planet blessed with an ocean."

Whole Story Comprehension *(cont.)*

Directions: After you have read the story on the previous page, answer the questions below.

1. How much of the earth's surface is covered by water?

   a. 97%

   b. 75%

   c. 10%

   d. nearly half

2. Sylvia Earle compares fishing trawlers to bulldozers because

   a. trawlers push the fish to the boats.

   b. they are both motorized equipment.

   c. trawlers are useful in creating new habitats for fish.

   d. as the trawlers are pulled along the ocean floor, they knock down whatever is in their way.

3. What earned Sylvia Earle the title "Her Deepness"?

   a. She lived in an underwater lab for two weeks.

   b. She walked freely on the ocean's floor without scuba equipment.

   c. Without a submarine, she has dived deeper than any other person.

   d. She works in the deep ocean every day.

4. What type of threat do trawlers pose to the ocean?

   a. They destroy natural habitats.

   b. They over-fish the oceans.

   c. They cause underwater gas leaks.

   d. both a and b

5. Sylvia Earle believes

   a. ocean exploration is important to the earth's future.

   b. space exploration is useless.

   c. more people should move close to the ocean.

   d. all of the above

6. Marine sanctuaries

   a. are used for commercial fishing.

   b. protect fish and their habitats.

   c. are underwater parks.

   d. hold 10 million to 30 million species of fish.

7. Why do you think 10 million to 30 million species of sea life are undiscovered?

   a. Some species are very small, even microscopic.

   b. They live in water too deep and too dark to be explored.

   c. They are in locations that cannot be safely explored by humans.

   d. All of the above answers are reasonable guesses.

8. What can be done to eliminate what Earle believes to be the greatest threat to the ocean?

   a. Ban fertilizers because killing large numbers of fish is the greatest threat.

   b. Limit commercial fishing because overuse of fishing grounds is the greatest threat.

   c. Educate ourselves about the link between the ocean and life on Earth because ignorance is the greatest threat.

   d. Learn to SCUBA dive because the lack of aquanauts is the greatest threat.

Enrichment

Directions: Read the information given in the box below. Then read each numbered sentence and choose the question that corresponds to each statement.

One way a writer makes a subject more interesting to a reader is by including specific numbers. Readers not only like to know when something happens, but also answers to questions such as "how much?" and "how many?"   Even if the exact number is not known, we can always approximate the information by adding the words "at least" or "more than." With dates, we can say "earlier than" or "later than."

When we use numbers in our writing, usually we spell out numbers one to ten. If we start a sentence with a number, we spell out that number, too. But the way numbers are written depends upon a style guide. Along with a lot of other information, a style guide gives instructions for how numbers should be written. Every newspaper uses a style guide. In your classroom, your English book or your teacher is the style guide.

Statements	**Questions**
_____ 1. In 1979, Earle was first called "Her Deepness."	a) when?
_____ 2. She walked on the ocean floor 1,250 feet beneath the water surface.	b) how long?
_____ 3. Oceans cover 75% of the planet Earth.	c) how many?
_____ 4. Half of the world's population lives close to the sea.	d) how old?
_____ 5. Henry was about eight years old when he left his country.	e) how far?
_____ 6. The volunteers had collected over $1,500 for charity.	f) how much?
_____ 7. One hundred teachers were surveyed by the Board of Education.	g) how heavy?
_____ 8. The survey discovered that the briefcases teachers carried averaged 20 pounds.	
_____ 9. Forty tons of paint are used each year to paint the Eiffel Tower.	
_____ 10. The top of the Eiffel Tower sways about four inches in a strong wind.	

Graphic Development

Directions: Use the chart below to answer the following questions.

Ocean	Average Depth (fathoms)	Deepest Point (fathoms)
Arctic	658.83 fathoms	Eurasia Basin, 2,980.17 fathoms
Atlantic	2,146.83 fathoms	Puerto Rico Trench, 4,705.16 fathoms
Indian	2,167 fathoms	Java Trench, 4,224 fathoms
Pacific	2,535.83 fathoms	Mariana Trench, 6,033.33 fathoms

One fathom = 6 feet

1. Which ocean has the greatest average depth?

   a. Arctic Ocean

   b. Atlantic Ocean

   c. Indian Ocean

   d. Pacific Ocean

2. Which ocean has the deepest point?

   a. Arctic Ocean

   b. Atlantic Ocean

   c. Indian Ocean

   d. Pacific Ocean

3. What unit of measure is used to denote nautical depth?

   a. feet

   b. yards

   c. fathoms

   d. miles

4. Based on the chart, what do you think *trench* means?

   a. ditch

   b. swimming area

   c. sea

   d. location

5. What is the best title that describes the contents of the chart?

   a. Ocean Sizes

   b. All About Oceans

   c. Ocean Depths

   d. Fathom That!

Sentence Comprehension

Directions: Read the sentence carefully and answer the following questions "True" (T) or "False" (F).

Today, instead of working in a courtroom, Schwarz skateboards around two pinball machines, a toy showroom, a Dalmatian named Kirby, and 21 employees at Rumpus' New York City headquarters.

1. The name of Schwarz's company is Kirby. _____

2. Schwarz works in New York City. _____

3. Schwarz skateboards to work because he doesn't have a car. _____

4. Apparently Schwarz is qualified to work in a courtroom. _____

5. Rumpus is the name of a law firm. _____

Word Study

Directions: Read the information given below and use it to answer the following questions "True" (T) or "False" (F).

Rumpus

Rumpus is a noun first used in 1764 to describe a noisy commotion, or a free-for-all with lots of noise and possible quarrels and violence. A person could still be arrested today if caught in a rumpus. In the mid-20th century, the word also became an adjective to describe a room. The rumpus room was usually in the basement of a house where games were played and parties were held. Today, Rumpus is the name of a toy company that makes inventive and playful toys, that promote good feelings. The way the meaning of rumpus has evolved shows that the meanings of words can change over time.

1. Rumpus can be used as a noun and an adjective. _____

2. Today, you could be arrested if involved in a rumpus. _____

3. Meanings of words change from century to century. _____

4. Rumpus comes from the verb "to roam." _____

5. A rumpus can take place only in the basement of a house. _____

Paragraph Comprehension

Directions: Read the paragraph below and use it to answer the following questions.

Larry Schwarz, 29, has tinkered with toys all his life. As a child, he would pull apart his toys, then glue a mishmash of the parts together. He'd make toy rockets, cars, and buildings out of boxes. Although he put his toys away long enough to become a child actor, a stand-up comic, and even a lawyer, nothing could shake Schwarz's childhood passion. In 1997, he started the Rumpus Toy Company, where he invents all the toys.

1. Schwarz is the founder of

   a. Tinkered Toys.

   b. a toy company.

   c. a rocket company.

   d. all of the above

2. Of all of Schwarz's careers, which goes back to a childhood love?

   a acting

   b. inventing

   c. comedy

   d. law

3. In this paragraph, *tinkered* means

   a. played with and altered.

   b loved.

   c. destroyed.

   d. banged on.

4. When did Larry Schwarz start his own company?

   a. as an adult

   b. as a child

   c. at age 29

   d. 1997

5. In the 1950s, people used the term "rumpus room" to describe a room in their home. Schwarz named his toy company Rumpus. What do you think *rumpus* means in this case?

   a. active play

   b. noisy commotion

   c. party

   d. hobby

Whole Story Comprehension

Directions: Read the story below and use it to answer the questions on the following page.

Serious About Fun

Larry Schwarz, 29, has tinkered with toys all his life. As a child, he would pull apart his toys, then glue a mishmash of the parts together. He'd make toy rockets, cars, and buildings out of boxes. Although he put his toys away long enough to become a child actor, a stand-up comic, and even a lawyer, nothing could shake Schwarz's childhood passion. In 1997, he started the Rumpus Toy Company, where he invents all the toys.

Schwarz knows it takes guts to compete with giant toy companies like Mattel and Hasbro. That's why he invents wacky toys like Gus Gutz, a stuffed doll with 12 squishy vital organs and Sy Klops, a one-eyed doll.

"We try to create clever stuff we want to play with," says Schwarz. Even the boxes are playful. Printed outlines and instructions on some Rumpus toy boxes allow you to turn them into clubhouses, TV's, buses, or gliders.

Schwarz dreamed up many toys while in law school. Instead of taking notes in class, he filled 26 notebooks with toy sketches! Still, he managed to get his law degree. Today, instead of working in a courtroom, Schwarz skateboards around two pinball machines, a toy showroom, a Dalmatian named Kirby, and 21 employees at Rumpus' New York City headquarters. The youngest worker is Tanner Zucker, 18, who oversees Rumpus' Web site, www.rumpustoys.com.

Schwarz loves to hit the highway in his Rumpus Road Rocket, a multicolored, retired school bus. He visits hospitals and schools, bringing toys, good cheer, and advice. Says Schwarz, "If you believe in something enough and think you can do it, you really should give it a try."

Whole Story Comprehension (cont.)

Directions: After you have read the story on the previous page, answer the questions below.

1. In what way does Rumpus Toys encourage recycling?

    a. by inventing new toys from old destroyed toys

    b. by skateboarding instead of using a car

    c. by bringing used toys to schools and hospitals

    d. by giving directions to turn toy boxes into playthings

2. How can you tell that Larry Schwarz was not very interested in becoming a lawyer?

    a. He was not paying attention in class.

    b. He brought toys to class.

    c. He failed to complete law school.

    d. He didn't go to class so he could play pinball.

3. Rumpus Toy Company

    a. is as big as Mattel and Hasbro.

    b. employs children.

    c. is the result of a man going after his dream.

    d. is suing Mattel for stealing the design for Gus Gutz.

4. Which paragraph from the story indicates that Larry Schwarz is generous?

    a. paragraph one

    b. paragraph three

    c. paragraph four

    d. paragraph five

5. Of the careers listed, which was not one of Schwarz's?

    a. bus driver

    b. actor

    c. comedian

    d. lawyer

6. Which saying do you think Larry Schwarz's story illustrates?

    a. "Dreams can come true."

    b. "Stay young at heart."

    c. "A penny saved is a penny earned."

    d. "Never tell a lie."

7. Which sentence is true?

    a. Larry Schwarz never graduated from law school.

    b. Larry Schwartz does nothing but play all day.

    c. Rumpus is a major manufacturer of pinball machines.

    d. Larry Schwarz has a dog in his headquarters.

8. Why does the article state that Larry Schwarz needs guts to be in his line of work?

    a. It is dangerous to skateboard in New York City.

    b. He owns a small toy company and there is a lot of competition from large toy companies.

    c. He invented a doll called Gus Gutz.

    d. He is responsible for paying 21 employees.

Enrichment

Directions: Read the information below and use it to answer the following questions "True" (T) or "False" (F).

Allusion

To explain a topic, an author sometimes uses words or terms that relate to a second topic. The author assumes that the readers have enough knowledge about that second subject to understand what is being talked about. When this is done, we call it an *allusion*. The author is *alluding* to the second subject. To *allude* to a subject means that an indirect reference is made to that subject. To *allude* literally means *to play*. Sometimes the author is playing with language in such a way that the reader might be amused.

In the article just read, Schwarz named a one-eyed doll Sy Klops. Schwarz is alluding to *The Odyssey*, a long story in which the hero, Odysseus, tricks a one-eyed monster, Cyclops, so that he and his men can escape being eaten. Another allusion is found in the name Gus Gutz. Unless the reader knows that another name for one's vital internal organs is "guts," the allusion would be missed. In both instances, Schwarz is playing with the sound of the words. He has spelled Cyclops as "Sy Klops" and guts as "gutz."

Note that an *allusion* is not the same as an *illusion*, something that deceives or misleads.

---

1. To allude only means playing with language. _____

2. "Gutz" is pronounced the same as "guts." _____

3. Odysseus had only one eye. _____

4. To understand an allusion, a reader needs to know a lot of different topics. _____

5. Allusion uses only direct references to a second topic. _____

6. Sy Klops was a monster found in *The Odyssey*. _____

7. Odysseus ate his men. _____

8. Odysseus saved his men from being eaten by Cyclops. _____

9. When Schwarz names some of his toys, he is playing with the sound of words. _____

10. To understand an allusion, we need to understand how illusions work. _____

Graphic Development

Directions: Read the information given below and use the items in the list to fill in the missing blanks on the map.

One way to organize information is by using a diagram. The diagram below is called a map. In the center of the map, you will find the most general word, toys. On this map, toys can be divided into our different types. Each line moving out from the center of the map represents one type of toy. In the four circles at the end of each line are the names of specific toys according to their type.

Not all of the lines have names on them and not all of the circles are filled in. Use the items in the list below to fill in the missing blanks on the map.

The Map

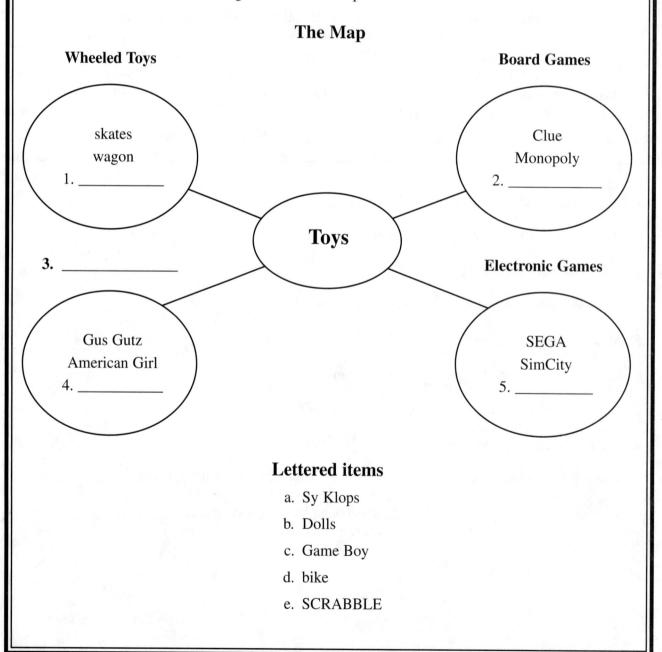

Lettered items

     a. Sy Klops

     b. Dolls

     c. Game Boy

     d. bike

     e. SCRABBLE

Sentence Comprehension

Directions: Read the sentence carefully and answer the following questions "True" (T) or "False" (F).

> The huge bay windows and rickety construction of the cottage interior wouldn't offer safety from high winds.

1. There has probably been dangerous weather predicted. _____

2. The cottage offers a safe haven from the storm. _____

3. The bay windows could pose a threat to the writer's well being. _____

4. *Rickety* indicates the cottage is old and run-down. _____

5. *High winds* can only mean a hurricane is approaching. _____

Word Study

Directions: Read the information given below and use it to answer the following questions "True" (T) or "False" (F).

> **Motel**
>
> *Motel* is a word made from a blend of two words, motor and hotel. When motor cars first became popular in the early twentieth century, people would sometimes travel long distances. When they needed to stay overnight, instead of going to a hotel where they might not find a place to park the car, they would go to a motel. A motel not only provided lodging for people, but also a place to park a car in front of a room. The first motel rooms were not joined as they are today. Instead, each room was in an individual cottage.

1. A motel only provides a place to park a car. _____

2. Motels were only found in the early 20th century. _____

3. Motel rooms were always joined. _____

4. People started to travel long distances by car in the early 20th century. _____

5. In this paragraph, *lodging* means a temporary place to stay for the night. _____

Paragraph Comprehension

Directions: Read the paragraph below and answer the following questions.

> The waterspout literally skipped. And then, like a monster of the night that is exposed to the sun, this monster of water began to disintegrate when it hit land. By the time it reached our cottage, it was nothing more than a strong gust of water-colored wind that pelted our bodies. The rest of the storm raged for an hour and then simply blew away.

1. Choose the best meaning for *disintegrate*.

    a. melt

    b. break apart

    c. blow away

    d. gust

2. How did the waterspout move toward the house?

    a. It blew.

    b. It pelted.

    c. It skipped.

    d. all of the above

3. What is compared to a "monster of the night"?

    a. the wind

    b. the cottage

    c. the sun

    d. the waterspout

4. This "monster of the night" is to the sun as "the waterspout" is to

    a. the land.

    b. the monster.

    c. the cottage.

    d. the storm.

5. Did the waterspout hit the cottage?

    a. Yes, but weakly.

    b. No, but a storm occurred.

    c. Yes, but everyone lived.

    d. No, the storm prediction was wrong.

Whole Story Comprehension

Directions: Read the story below and answer the questions on the following page.

Race the Wind

When the sand began kicking up and lashing our faces, I started to worry that maybe we had made a mistake. Maybe we should have left the beach.

That afternoon, my dad had stood on the deck of our home and laughed as our neighbors packed up their cars and headed inland. They left to spend the night in motels or at friends' homes that were out of range of the approaching summer storm. My dad believed his family was made of stronger stuff.

Challenging the weather that threatened to dampen our spirits, my sister, my mom, and I lit a fire on the beach. Dad told jokes and used sticks as skewers to roast marshmallows that tasted like the burned bark.

Now, it was 6:30 P.M. and all laughter evaporated. Our eyes were drawn to the sky. A dark wall of clouds marched toward us. The red sunset bled through the storm clouds, turning the sky into a swirling torrent of dark fire. Below, the black waters of Lake Michigan grappled and slammed against each other as they sent icy tendrils toward the sky. Both sky and lake appeared locked in a dangerous battle, and we were trapped in the middle.

"Look!" My sister, Kim, spotted it first. Her tiny finger pointed toward the horizon. It was a waterspout, a tornado whose funnel was made of fresh water. It was headed straight for us.

In a flash, we were all on our feet. My dad began mumbling, "It's okay, it's okay." The wind started screaming and now we were running to the cottage. My mom stopped next to the front door. "Where can we go?" She shouted the question at my dad.

Most cottages on this part of Lake Michigan had been built without basements. Ours was no exception. The huge bay windows and rickety construction of the cottage interior wouldn't offer safety from high winds.

I turned to look at the sky. Now it didn't look beautiful. It looked deadly. This liquid sister of the tornado wouldn't wait for us to get in the car and drive to safety.

"Under the deck!" my dad yelled. We scrambled beneath the deck, pressing ourselves against the foundation of the cottage. Between the deck supports, we watched the approaching storm in silent terror.

The 200-foot-high waterspout shot toward us, not in the lazy way of a wave, but as if it had been fired from a cannon the size of the sun.

My dad shouted, "Hold on!" and something else I couldn't hear over the screaming wind. I think he was praying.

The spout sprinted over the final stretch of water, an animal eager to make the kill. It lunged over the crashing waves. It twisted through the blood-red sky, and then it hit the beach.

The waterspout literally skipped. And then, like a monster of the night that is exposed to the sun, this monster of water began to disintegrate when it hit land. By the time it reached our cottage, it was nothing more than a strong gust of water-colored wind that pelted our bodies. The rest of the storm raged for an hour and then simply blew away.

"Next time, we'll stay inland at Grandma's. Okay?" my dad said, tears of relief in his eyes. We all agreed that it would be a good idea.

Whole Story Comprehension *(cont.)*

Directions: After you have read the story on the previous page, answer the questions below.

1. How many people are braving the storm?

     a. two

     b. three

     c. four

     d. five

2. Who first spotted the waterspout?

     a. Dad

     b. Mom

     c. the narrator

     d. Kim

3. What is called "the liquid sister of a tornado"?

     a. the blood red sky

     b. the waterspout

     c. the water-colored wind

     d. Kim

4. Which word does not give the reader the feeling of the storm's intensity?

     a. screaming

     b. deadly

     c. lunged

     d. dampen

5. Where does the family go for safety from the storm?

     a. in the cottage

     b. away from the beach

     c. under the deck

     d. in the basement

6. In paragraph 10, what does the author mean by "as if it had been fired from a cannon the size of the sun"?

     a. It was powerful and fast moving.

     b. It was spherical, like a cannon ball.

     c. It was heading straight for them.

     d. It was dangerous.

7. What caused the waterspout to lose power?

     a. strong gusts of wind

     b. hitting land

     c. crashing waves

     d. the final stretch of water

8. What is the opposite of *fear*?

     a. apprehension

     b. terror

     c. anxiety

     d. relief

Enrichment

Directions: Read the information below and use it to answer the following questions.

Personification

The writer of this article used many interesting verbs to make the story come alive.

The sand "kicks up" and "lashes." A wall of clouds "marches." The sunset "bleeds." Waves "grapple" and "slam." The wind "screams." The spout "sprints." It "lunges," "twists," and "skips."

The writer thinks of these natural elements as living creatures. We call this way of writing personification. *Personification* is a figure of speech that gives animals, ideas, and non-living objects or ideas personality and emotions. The writer of "Race the Wind" even calls the waterspout "an animal eager for a kill" and "a monster of water."

In the sentences below, if the sentence contains personification, write "Yes" (Y); if it does not contain personification, write "No" (N).

1. April shakes out her rain-soaked hair. _____

2. October is a very windy month. _____

3. War shook his angry fist at the poor peasants. _____

4. Peace is hard to achieve. _____

5. The rosy-fingered dawn smiles at the sailor. _____

6. Soccer is the king of sports. _____

7. Danger knows that we are scared. _____

8. Horseracing is the sport of kings. _____

9. She was cool from sleep. _____

10. The rain strikes and bites me. _____

Graphic Development

Directions: Use the information in the chart given below to choose the letter that best identifies the wind strength seen in the following situations.

Tornado Strength Chart

Strength	Wind Speed (MPH)	Damage	Percent
F0	40–77	Shattered windows, broken branches	69%
F1	73–112	Rips shingles from roofs, moves mobile homes	29%
F2	113–157	Trees uprooted, mobile homes destroyed, roofs lifted off	
F3	158–206	Turns over cars, blows down walls of houses	2%
F4	207–260	Destroys homes, lifts and carries large objects	
F5	260+	Lifts homes off of foundations, damages steel structures	

Possible Wind Strengths

a. FO   b. F1   c. F2   d. F3   e. F4   f. F5

Situations

_____ 1. "The damage was devastating! I saw my car lifted right off the ground. The 240 MPH winds turned my home into a heap of rubble."

_____ 2. "We heard the warnings and went right to the basement. We feel fortunate that our neighborhood only suffered some broken tree limbs. The damage was very light."

_____ 3. "When the tornado hit, it sounded like a freight train. The destruction was severe. Cars were turned over in the street. Reports say the wind speed was up to 180 miles per hour."

_____ 4. "The tornado hit the Serenity Mobile Home Park. Many of the mobile homes were destroyed. Trees were uprooted. The Red Cross will arrive by nightfall."

_____ 5. "I lost most of the shingles on my garage roof. My lawn furniture was tossed around the yard."

Sentence Comprehension

Directions: Read the sentence carefully and answer the following questions "True" (T) or "False" (F).

> I imagined French experts dropping from helicopters in a desperate attempt to free their beloved Tower from the crushing hug of this tiny American.

1. Helicopters actually arrived to save the Tower. _____

2. A tiny American was attempting to free the Tower. _____

3. The tiny American was desperate in an attempt to be free from the tower. _____

4. The Tower is liked very much by the French experts. _____

5. The American was crushed by the helicopters. _____

Word Study

Directions: Read the information given below and use it to answer the following questions "True" (T) or "False" (F).

> **Panic**
>
> *Panic* is a word that means fright. When *panicked*, a person can be so frightened that the mind goes blank. A *panic* button is a button that is supposed to be pushed in case of an emergency.
>
> *Panic* has a second meaning. Sometimes when a person does something very, very funny, we call that person a *panic*.
>
> *Panic* is an emotional state supposedly caused by the Greek god, Pan. The top half of Pan's body was a man's, but his bottom half was like the bottom half of a goat. As he walked on his goat's feet, he played the Pipes of Pan, a wind instrument made of hollow reeds of different lengths. Unfortunately, Pan scared people with his appearance and his behavior and caused them to rush away in a *panic*.

1. John is a panic when he tells funny jokes. _____

2. When we are in a panic, we always know the reason for our fright. _____

3. The Greek god, Pan, walked on all fours like a goat. _____

4. When spelling the past tense of *to panic*, we need to drop the "c" and add a "k." _____

5. The Greek god, Pan, told many funny jokes that made people like him. _____

Paragraph Comprehension

Directions: Read the paragraph below and answer the following questions.

The elevator door slid open. The crowd inside let out a collective gasp of excitement. But no one was more excited than my mom. This 110-pound woman is not normally rude, but suddenly she had all the courtesy of a linebacker diving for a fumble. My mom charged through the door, nearly knocking over an elderly German tourist.

1. Where did the elevator stop?

   a. at the top

   b. at the bottom

   c. in the middle

   d. There is not enough information to tell.

2. The author compares her mother to

   a. a 110-pound woman.

   b. a German tourist.

   c. a linebacker.

   d. a fumble.

3. Which sentence can we be sure is true?

   a. The author and her mom were not alone in the elevator.

   b. Everyone thought her mom was rude.

   c. The German tourist was an elderly woman.

   d. A football player was on the elevator.

4. Which word is a synonym for *courtesy*?

   a. gasp

   b. rude

   c. mannerly

   d. collective

5. By her mother's behavior, we can guess that

   a. she was happy to get out of the elevator.

   b. she was excited to see her destination.

   c. she wanted to get out quickly.

   d. all of the above

Whole Story Comprehension

Directions: Read the story below and use it to answer the questions on the following page.

Panic in Paris

The elevator door slid open. The crowd inside let out a collective gasp of excitement. But no one was more excited than my mom. This 110-pound woman is not normally rude, but suddenly she had all the courtesy of a linebacker diving for a fumble. My mom charged through the door, nearly knocking over an elderly German tourist.

My mom wasn't interested in the sights; she just wanted air. If there's one thing that frightens my mom more than cramped spaces, it's heights. We were now 889 feet above the Paris cityscape. Maybe we should have taken the Eiffel Tower off our "to do" list.

By the time I caught up with her, she had pressed her entire body against a huge steel girder that zigzagged through the structure. The Eiffel Tower was her giant teddy bear. I couldn't help but laugh.

"What?" she said defensively, her arms wrapped around the support and her face flushed. "I'm having a great time."

"Yeah, I can tell. Let's go," I said.

My mom replied, "I can't." Amidst the twinkling reflection of the City of Lights, I saw terror in her eyes. She was so scared of heights, she couldn't move. I imagined French experts dropping from helicopters in a desperate attempt to free their beloved Tower from the crushing hug of this tiny American.

I was going to have to think of something—and fast. "I know, Mom!" I shouted, making her jump. "We don't have to get back in the elevator. We can walk all the way down." Before she could think about it, I took her arm and led her over to the stairs.

Hoping to distract her, I pulled out our Paris guidebook and called out facts about the Tower as we made our way down. There are a total of 1,652 steps. Forty tons of paint are used on the Tower every year. The Tower sways about four inches in strong winds.

Finally, after 20 minutes, we headed down the last flight. "See? That wasn't so bad."

I pushed on the steel exit gate. The gate didn't move. I felt a twinge of panic. I pushed again, still no movement. Were we trapped? My hands repositioned for better leverage. I shoved again and again against the gate. Out of breath, I felt on the verge of tears. I hated being locked in. What was wrong with the door?

"Qu'est-ce que c'est la probleme?"

A young French security guard stood on the other side of the gate. He repeated his question. The fact that I didn't understand French only made me panic more. I banged violently on the door, and rocked against it—still nothing.

The guard smiled now. He pointed up and said in English, "The sign. Read it."

I followed his pointing finger to a sign that hung above the gate. It said: "Tirez." I looked at the guard blankly. What did that mean?

"The sign," the guard told me. "It says, *Pull.*"

Stepping back, I stopped pushing the gate. I pulled instead. It swung open easily on greased hinges. Now my face burned with embarrassment, not panic.

"Karen, you really need to learn to relax," my mom said, laughing as she breezed past me.

Whole Story Comprehension *(cont.)*

Directions: After you have read the story on the previous page, answer the questions below.

1. Which word or phrase indicates there were people from more than one country on the elevator?

    a. Paris

    b. guidebook

    c. international

    d. guard

2. Karen's mom suffers from two fears. What are they?

    a. fear of elevators and crowds

    b. fear of heights and crowded places

    c. fear of flying and strangers

    d. fear of twinkling lights and steel girders

3. Which fact from the guidebook did not distract Karen's mom from her fear?

    a. There are 1,652 steps in the Eiffel Tower.

    b. It sways four inches on windy days.

    c. The Tower is made of steel.

    d. Forty tons of paint per year are used on the Eiffel Tower.

4. What triggered Karen's fear?

    a. She couldn't understand the guard's directions.

    b. She couldn't read the sign.

    c. The Tower started to sway.

    d. She thought she was locked in.

5. *Tirez* is the French word for

    a. sign.

    b. open.

    c. push.

    d. pull.

6. By using clues from the story, guess the meaning of "Que'est-ce que c'est la probleme"?

    a. There is a problem with the gate.

    b. What is the problem?

    c. What are you crying for?

    d. Where are you going?

7. Choose the title that would not be an appropriate alternative to the present title.

    a. Tower of Terror

    b. Frightened in France

    c. Landmark of Laughter

    d. Tower Tour for a Timid Twosome

8. New York is called the Big Apple. In the article, Paris is called _____

    a. Cityscape.

    b. City of Lights.

    c. Gay Paris.

    d. Tirez.

Enrichment

Directions: Read the information below and use it to match the words and the definitions.

Phobias

The mother in this story is afraid of heights. Years ago, in ancient Greece, doctors called a fear like this a "phobia." A phobia is an abnormal fear of a particular object or situation, usually without adequate cause. Karen's mom has *acrophobia* or a fear of heights. Another phobia shared by many people is *aerophobia* or a fear of flying. Some people cannot cross bridges because they have *gephyrophobia*.

Many small children have *nyctophobia* and must sleep with a light on. Or they are frightened of seeing blood because they have *hemophobia*. *Triskaidekaphobia* is a fear of the number 13. But imagine trying to do your arithmetic homework if you had *numerophobia*!

Some people are afraid of certain objects. *Arachnophobia* is a fear of spiders, *aquaphobia* is a fear of water, *cynophobia* is a fear of dogs, *herpetophobia* is a fear of reptiles, and *murophobia* is a fear of mice.

Doctors do not always know what causes a phobia, but having one sometimes causes an individual to have difficulty doing things that most of us take for granted. Imagine what your life would be like if you have *agoraphobia* or a fear of open spaces. You would be frightened to go into an open field. If you had *claustrophobia* or a fear of being in a confined space, you could never go into your closet without feeling panicked. And say goodbye to peanut butter and jelly sandwiches if you have a fear of peanut butter sticking to the roof of your mouth or *archibutyrophobia*.

Definitions

1. a fear of the number 13 _____

2. a fear of flying _____

3. a fear of crossing bridges _____

4. a fear of open spaces _____

5. a fear of dogs _____

6. a fear of water _____

7. a fear of being in a confined space _____

8. a fear of numbers _____

9. a fear of the dark _____

10. a fear of heights _____

Words

a. acrophobia

b. aerophobia

c. gephyrophobia

d. nyctophobia

e. hemophobia

f. numerophobia

g. arachnophobia

h. trishkaikaphobia

i. aquaphobia

j. cynophobia

k. herpetophobia

l. murophobia

m. agoraphobia

n. claustrophobia

o. archibutrophobia

Graphic Development

Directions: Look carefully at the map of Paris and write if the statements are "True" (T) or "False" (F).

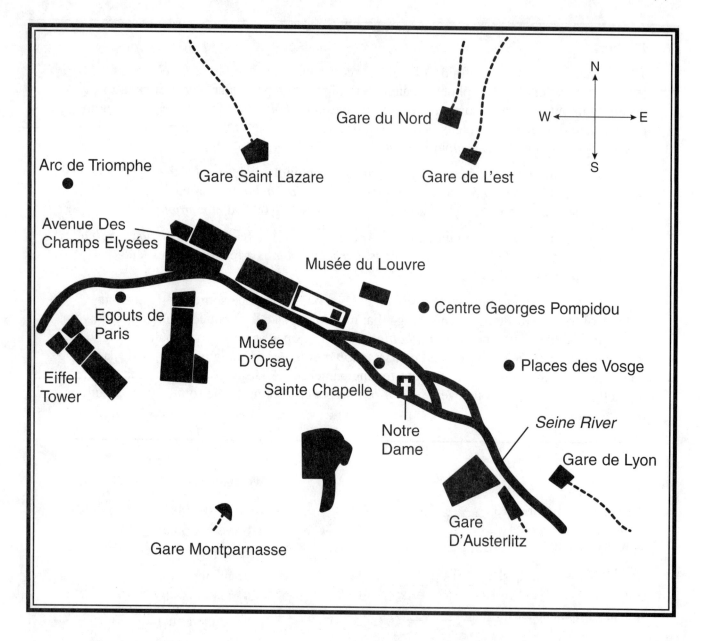

1. To visit the Eiffel Tower from the Arc de Triomphe walk southeast. _____

2. Musée du Louvre is north of Notre Dame Cathedral. _____

3. Travel northeast along the Seine to get from the Eiffel Tower to the Louvre. _____

4. Notre Dame Cathedral is on an island in the middle of the Seine River. _____

5. *Gare* means train station. Paris has six train stations. _____

Sentence Comprehension

Directions: Read the sentence carefully and answer the following questions "True" (T) or "False" (F).

> Wang and his wife are just two of the 1.2 million Chinese who are being forced from their homes by the construction of the Three Gorges Dam.

1. Wang wants to move to live closer to the Three Gorges Dam. _____

2. The Chinese are being paid 1.2 million dollars to relocate. _____

3. The word *forced* indicates the Wangs are not happy about the move. _____

4. The Three Gorges Dam will be located in China. _____

5. Part of the dam will be built on land where people have homes. _____

Word Study

Directions: Read the information given below and use it to answer the following questions "True" (T) or "False" (F).

> The Three Gorges are three very narrow steep-walled canyons on the Yangtze River.
>
> Any river could have a *gorge*. Not all *gorges* have water running through them at the present time, but they are usually formed by water wearing away stone over a long period of time. A narrow entrance to a fort is also called a *gorge*.
>
> *Gorge* also means throat. It is possible to see the connection between these two meanings. The throat is a narrow passage through which food goes. A *gorge* on the Yangtze River is a narrow passage though which water goes. In both cases, food or water is sucked through a narrow passage. *Gorge* actually comes from a Latin word meaning whirlpool, but it does not mean that today.
>
> *Gorge* is also a verb that means to eat greedily. If you have eaten so many French fries that you are about to burst, you have *gorged* yourself. Also, if an object is so filled with a liquid that it is about to burst, it is said to be *gorged*. After we filled the balloon with water, we could say the balloon was *gorged* with water.

1. Gorge can mean canyon. _____

2. Gorge can mean throat. _____

3. Gorge can mean whirlpool. _____

4. Gorge can mean about to burst. _____

5. Gorge can mean a fort. _____

Paragraph Comprehension

Directions: Read the paragraph below and use it to answer the following questions.

Workers are building a 600-foot-high wall that will stretch across the Yangtze. Then they will install giant generators. These will provide as much energy for the area as 15 large coal-burning power stations. However, many scientists say the dam will be an ecological disaster. It will destroy the natural surroundings (including the studding gorges) and threaten many fish and animals.

---

1. The *Yangtze* is

    a. a river.

    b. a reservoir.

    c. a lake.

    d. a wall.

2. At the present time, before the generators are installed, energy comes from

    a. water.

    b. Yinchang.

    c. coal-burning power stations.

    d. natural sources.

3. In what way will this cause an ecological disaster?

    a. People will have to move.

    b. Fish and other animals will die.

    c. It will create a lake.

    d. People will have to burn more coal.

4. The 600-foot-high wall will form

    a. a dam.

    b. a river.

    c. an ocean.

    d. a coal-burning power station.

5. How tall is the dam?

    a. as wide as the Yangtze

    b. 370 miles high

    c. 15 miles high

    d. 600 feet high

Whole Story Comprehension

Directions: Read the story below and use it to answer the questions on the following page.

China's Big Dam

Farmer Wang Zuolu grows oranges and peanuts on a hilltop overlooking China's beautiful Yangtze (Yang-zee) River. His family has lived there for generations in a farmhouse of thick, mud-packed walls. But Wang, 70, and his wife Zhang Changying, 60, know that their family's happy life on the hill is coming to an end. Soon their farm will be covered by water. They must start a new life in a new village. They will have to move their family cemetery and replant their orchards.

Wang and his wife are just two of the 1.2 million Chinese who are being forced from their homes by the construction of the Three Gorges Dam.

The Three Gorges Dam is named for three spectacular gorges, or canyons, in central China. When it is completed, the dam will use water power to create electricity. Its builders say it will help prevent flooding by the Yangtze. But it will also be very destructive, changing China's natural scenery and the lives of many of its people forever.

For hundreds of years, poets and painters have been inspired by the Yangtze's winding path and the steep cliffs and flat plains that lie on either side of its waters. But the Yangtze can rise over its banks, causing terrible floods.

Workers are building a 600-foot-high wall that will stretch across the Yangtze. Then they will install giant generators. These will provide as much energy for the area as 15 large coal-burning power stations. However, many scientists say the dam will be an ecological disaster. It will destroy the natural surroundings (including the studding gorges) and threaten many fish and animals.

By blocking the flow of the Yangtze, the dam will create a 370-mile lake, or reservoir, west of the city of Yinchang (Yee-chang). It will swallow hundreds of towns and villages.

The reservoir will also threaten the habitats of hundreds of fish, plants, and animal species. Among the creatures at risk: rare river dolphins, clouded leopards, and Siberian white cranes. The government promises to monitor the environment around the dam and has set aside money to create a protective area for the dolphins.

But scientists are doubtful about promises. They warn that blocking the river will create sewage backups and perhaps even cause more floods. Some fear that the dam may collapse. Many dams in China have collapsed in the past 20 years.

China's culture and history are also endangered by the dam. Ancient pagodas (temples) and other important historic sites will be under water.

The Chinese who must leave their homes are already feeling the impact of the Three Gorges Dam. These resettlers, or yimin (yee-min), have no choice but to find new homes and jobs.

Despite their worries, the Chinese are not permitted to speak out against the project, which is expected to cost more than $24 billion. Journalist Dai Qing landed in prison after she criticized the dam. "There is only one Yangtze River," she wrote in protest. "And we have already subjected it to many stupid deeds."

Whole Story Comprehension (cont.)

Directions: After you have read the story on the previous page, answer the questions below.

1. A *gorge* is another name for a

   a. valley.

   b. canyon.

   c. dam.

   d. river.

2. Why is the Three Gorges Dam being created?

   a. to create electricity

   b. to change China's natural scenery

   c. to create a protective area for dolphins

   d. to protect pagodas and temples

3. Which word or phrase does not describe Wang?

   a. farmed oranges and peanuts

   b. lived on a hilltop

   c. a yimin

   d. husband of Dai Qing

4. By building a dam, the Yangtze will

   a. create a reservoir where towns and villages used to be.

   b. endanger historic sites and pagodas.

   c. generate power.

   d. all of the above

5. Why don't the 1.2 million people refuse to leave?

   a. They know the dam will be good for the country.

   b. They might be sent to prison.

   c. They want a change of scenery.

   d. Their homes are old and run-down.

6. What animals will be placed in a government-funded protected area?

   a. clouded leopards

   b. Siberian white cranes

   c. pagodas

   d. rare river dolphins

7. What does a journalist do?

   a. protests

   b. reports the news

   c. sells homes

   d. advises the government

8. Why do some people fear the dam will collapse?

   a. Many of China's dams have collapsed in the past.

   b. They are poorly constructed.

   c. The river is too strong.

   d. The people will knock it down in protest.

Enrichment

Directions: Read the information below and use it to tell if the following statements are "True" (T) or "False" (F).

Taoist and "Wu-wei"

Many years ago, in ancient China, there was an emperor who was very concerned about a large river that flooded each spring and caused many of his people to die. He called before him two of his most experienced engineers and asked what could be done to solve the problem of the floods.

The first engineer said that he would build a large dam. The dam would hold back the water that rushed through the gorges when the snows melted. Of course, the dam would cause a big lake and some villagers would have to be relocated; their temples and graveyards would have to be moved. But there would be no more mudslides, villages would be spared, and the water could be used to irrigate the crops during the dry season.

The second engineer said that he would dig a long canal that would divert the water from the river in such a way that further downstream, where the river bed was wider, the two would become one. No dam needed to be built, the gorges would remain natural, and there would be no artificial lake. He also said that there would be no mudslides, villages would be spared, and no families or cemeteries would have to be moved. The water in the river and the canal could still be used to irrigate the crops.

The emperor listened carefully to each engineer. Then he awarded the second engineer for his wisdom. He had the first engineer executed for his plan to disrupt nature.

The emperor was a Taoist (pronounced Dow-ist). Taoism is an ancient Chinese philosophy first popular in the third and fourth centuries. A Taoist believed that man should be natural and spontaneous and seek simplicity. A central idea of its beliefs was *wu-wei*. "Wu-wei" is an action that does not force but yields. For example, under the weight of a heavy snowfall, some trees break. But by bending its branches, a tree like the willow can get rid of the snow and not break. Water is an excellent symbol of wu-wei because it is soft and yielding, yet it is able to cut through hard rock. In other words, Taoism says that one should follow the action that is most natural.

---

1. The emperor wanted to build a dam. _____

2. The emperor probably lived during the first or second century. _____

3. The first engineer was rewarded by the emperor. _____

4. The dam would keep the gorges natural. _____

5. The Taoists philosophers thought water was a hard substance. _____

6. The emperor gave prizes to both engineers. _____

7. The emperor was a Taoist. _____

8. An action that yields like a willow tree under snow is a wu-wei action. _____

9. The second engineer was going to dig a long canal to take some of the flood water away from the river bed. _____

10. Both engineers promised the emperor that there would be no more mudslides. _____

Graphic Development

Directions: Look carefully at the map that shows the section of the Yangtze River that will be affected by the Three Gorges Dam and tell if the statements are "True" (T) or "False" (F).

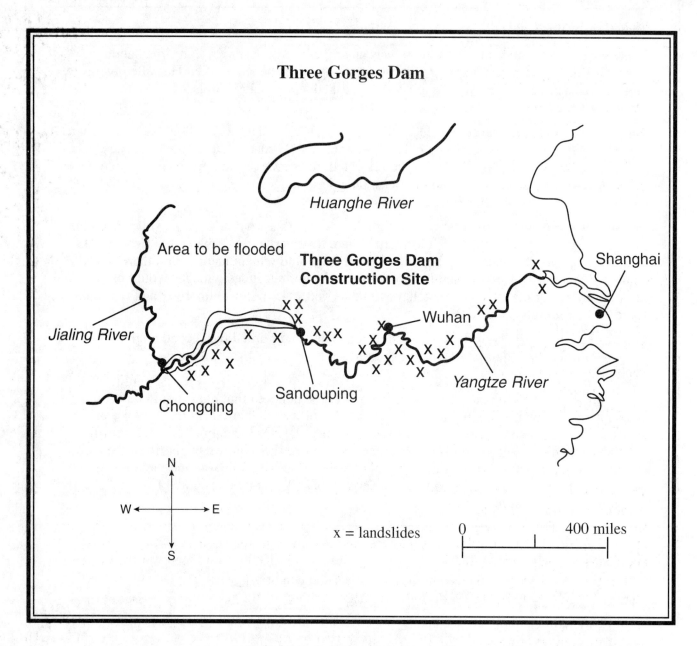

1. Approximately 400 miles of the Yangtze will be affected by the dam. _____

2. Chonguing has been affected by landslides. _____

3. Most of the cities are on the south side of the river. _____

4. The Yangtze flows east. _____

5. Shanghai is southeast of Wuhan. _____

Sentence Comprehension

Directions: Read the sentence carefully and answer the following questions "True" (T) or "False" (F).

This software prevents access to many areas on the Internet, including sites dealing with art, literature, women's health, politics, religion, and free speech.

---

1. The software gives access to some Internet sites. _____

2. Art sites can be seen. _____

3. Sites about politics are forbidden. _____

4. The Internet does not have sites about free speech. _____

5. Some software protects people on the Internet. _____

Word Study

Directions: Read the information given below and use the information about slanted language to help you tell if the adjective makes you feel "Positively" (P) or "Negatively" (N) about the object described.

Slanted Language

Each of the two articles that you are about to read is trying to persuade you about the way the Internet should be used in public libraries. One claims that there should be free access, and the other claims that blocks should be placed on the Internet so that certain sites would not be available.

When writers are trying to get their readers to agree with their viewpoints, they use reasons and facts to support their arguments. Sometimes they also use *slanted language*.

The writer of the second article says that kids should be protected from vicious predators. A *predator* is usually an animal that obtains its food by killing and consuming other animals. A wolf is a predator as is a tiger. But the writer is not writing about animals; she is writing about people who, in her opinion, behave like animals in their treatment of children. These people do not eat children, but they injure and destroy children by using them for their own purposes. Predators are, by nature, vicious, so when she adds the adjective vicious, she is making her attack on such people doubly strong.

Even though you may agree with her statement, remember that she is still using *slanted language*. This is language that will cause the reader to feel positively or negatively about the subject because of the particular words that are used. Arguments based on slanted language are not as strong as those based on reasons and facts.

---

1. a stubborn donkey _____

2. a senior citizen _____

3. a mob of students _____

4. firm-minded principal _____

5. a slim girl _____

Paragraph Comprehension

Directions: Read the paragraph below and use it to answer the following questions.

> Most public libraries now offer all visitors—kids and adults alike—free access to all sites on the Internet. Just like any powerful tool, limits must be placed on it. After all, not all sites are good for children or appropriate for them. Some are violent. Some, in the name of free speech, say irresponsible things. Others feature incorrect information for research. And many should be labeled "For Adults Only."

1. Internet access is available to

    a. adults and children in most libraries.

    b. adults only in some libraries.

    c. some visitors in some libraries.

    d. children if they are accompanied by an adult.

2. Which statement is an opinion?

    a. Limits must be placed on Internet sites.

    b. Some public libraries offer free Internet access.

    c. The Internet is a source of information.

    d. Many libraries have computers.

3. The writer believes children should be

    a. encouraged to use the Internet freely.

    b. monitored while using the Internet to protect them from inappropriate sites.

    c. prevented from using powerful tools.

    d. exposed to violent and irresponsible Web sites.

4. What right of an American citizen would be violated if the Internet were censored?

    a. the right to vote

    b. the right to bear arms

    c. the right to pursue happiness

    d. the right to free speech

5. According to the paragraph, libraries must

    a. place limits on Internet access.

    b. allow free access to the Internet.

    c. charge children to enter adult Web sites.

    d. not allow any children to "surf the net."

Whole Story Comprehension

Directions: Read the two letters below and use them to answer the questions on the following page.

Should Kids Be Able to Surf the Internet?

Dear Editor,

Most public libraries now offer all visitors, kids and adults alike, free access to all sites on the Internet. Just like any powerful tool, limits must be placed on it. After all, not all sites are good for children or appropriate for them. Some are violent. Some, in the name of free speech, say irresponsible things. Others feature incorrect information for research. And many should be labeled "For Adults Only."

In 1998, there were 100,000 commercial adult sites on the Web, with as many as 200 new adult sites added each day. Couple this figure with the fact that there are roughly 200 million American children under the age 18 with Internet access, and you have a recipe for disaster.

Back in 1967, the American Library Association (ALA) passed a resolution that stated "a person's right to use a library should not be denied . . . because of origin, age, background, or views." Some groups argue that this resolution gives children the right to free and total access to the Internet and its unsuitable sites.

This resolution was fine in the past, but it never considered the birth of the Internet. Besides, the ALA isn't a government agency. It has no power to pass laws, and its resolutions are not legally binding.

We must pass real laws that tie U.S. government funds for library computers to the use of software that blocks out offensive material online. If the libraries don't use the software, then they don't get computers.

As a working parent, I can't be with my child every time he turns on the computer. I don't expect libraries to be babysitters. But I do expect them to work with me, not against me, in making sure my child is protected from adult-only and other irresponsible sites.

Sincerely,

Julie Richardson

Redding, California

Dear Editor,

What if, when our nation was pushing west, someone stepped forward at the Mississippi River and said, "Okay, that's far enough!" and we had stopped? We would never know the wonders that lay beyond.

Those who would restrict Internet access are threatening to destroy expansion on a similar scale. Of the nearly 9,000 public libraries in the United States, over 60 percent offer access to the Internet. But this learning tool could be seriously hampered by the increasing number of libraries using software to block access to certain Web sites.

Lawmakers were threatening the democratic mission of libraries by forcing them to use blocking software. This software prevents access to many areas on the Internet, including sites dealing with art, literature, women's health, politics, religion, and free speech.

Public libraries provide information to all, regardless of race, economic background, and age. What if you can't afford a home computer and your only choice is to use one of the library's? If this computer uses blocking software, then you are being denied the access that people with home computers have.

Obviously, we have to protect our kids from disturbing images and vicious predators. But that protection would come in the form of teaching, not preaching. As the American Civil Liberties Union suggests, we should start Drivers' Ed-type courses that show kids how to navigate the roads of the Internet. These classes would teach children to use critical thinking and reasoning skills to distinguish between what's valuable and what's trash. We should give our kids the tools they need to make the right decisions, not make the decisions for them. Let's not kill something before we understand it.

Sincerely yours,

Ali Hershey

Salisbury, Maryland

Whole Story Comprehension *(cont.)*

Directions: After you have read the story on the previous page, answer the questions below.

1. Julie Richardson wrote her letter

    a. to persuade the government to require inappropriate subjects to be blocked on the Internet.

    b. to ban Internet use in libraries.

    c. to agree with the ALA's 1967 resolution.

    d. to require adult supervision during Internet use.

2. The main idea of Ali Hershey's letter is that blocking software

    a. is necessary to protect children.

    b. denies users the right of free speech.

    c. denies users access to some appropriate and important information.

    d. protects children from only violent and disturbing sites.

3. In 1967,

    a. many households had Internet access.

    b. the Internet did not exist.

    c. children were not allowed in libraries.

    d. blocking software was popular.

4. Who wrote the letter against blocking software?

    a. Ali Hershey

    b. the editor

    c. Julie Richardson

    d. Redding

5. What is the term Julie Richardson used that means bad things are bound to happen?

    a. "an accident waiting to happen"

    b. "burning bridges"

    c. "six-to-one, half-dozen to another"

    d. "a recipe for disaster"

6. What does Julie Richardson consider as "unsuitable" for children?

    a. information about body parts

    b. information about violent events

    c. information unsuitable for every family

    d. information about weapons

7. What does Ali Hershey propose instead of blocking software?

    a. joining the American Civil Liberties Union

    b. boycotting the library

    c. restricting Internet access

    d. providing classes to teach children to make responsible decisions

8. Julie Richardson proposes that libraries must use blocking software or they will

    a. lose their computers.

    b. forfeit their funding for computers.

    c. close the library.

    d. be breaking the law.

Enrichment

Directions: Read the information below and match the terms with the meanings.

To use the Internet, it is helpful to know some special terms. The Internet, or "the Net" as some people call it, is a network that connects millions of computer users from all over the world. Through the Internet, we can get information from a variety of sources. We can also send and receive e-mail, or electronic mail. It is possible that you might be asked to access an electronic bulletin board to get the daily notices for your school.

"To surf," or cruise the net, means to wander around the Internet going from source to source, just to see what is there. This is similar to wandering in a library and looking at the shelves and occasionally pulling down a book to look at its contents.

Sometimes you can go to a search engine that will help you find exactly what you are looking for. The search engine will ask you to type in a question or a topic and then it will offer suggestions about where you can go next. Yahoo, Alta Vista, and Infoseek are a few search engines that are helpful. You will also find specialized "sites" or locations that are helpful for certain topics.

The "Web" or the World Wide Web is a large portion of the Internet that contains linked documents called pages. Any time you need to type in an address on the Internet, you need to place "www" (without the quotation marks) in front of the address.

A "homepage" is a document on the Web, which gives information about a person or an institution. If you like a particular homepage, it is possible to "bookmark" or save the address of the homepage so that you can go back to it without retyping the whole "www" address. You can also create your own homepage.

Something you do not want to do is "to flame" or to post e-mail or other messages that will insult or provoke another user. You also do not want to be a "hacker." This is someone who breaks into other peoples' programs and causes damage. Sometimes they will spread viruses which will destroy the material on your computer. Viruses sometimes come without you knowing about them from e-mail and attachments to e-mail.

Terms	**Meanings**
1. to flame	a. to save the address of a homepage
2. to bookmark	b. a place where you can find information about a person
3. homepage	c. a virus
4. www	d. a specific search engine
5. search engine	e. a person who deliberately tries to destroy other people's programs
6. Infoseek	f. a good starting point for finding information about your topic
7. Yahoo	g. to wander around the Internet with no particular purpose
8. e-mail	h. to post e-mail that will insult or provoke another user
9. to surf	i. electronic mail
10. hacker	j. World Wide Web

Graphic Development

Directions: Look carefully at the Internet Reference Guide. Each picture is called an "icon," a small image representing the type of information you will find at that link. Answer the following questions by choosing the correct letter of the link that would help you find the required information.

Internet Reference Guide

 a. Art/Music/Museums/Theater

 d. Earth Science/Animals/Insects/ Space/Dinosaurs

 b. Best Seller Lists/Meet the Author/Review/Fan Club Chat Room

 **e.** Baseball/Football/Basketball/ Soccer/X-Sports

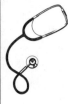 **c.** Anatomy & Physiology/Nutrition/ Exercise/Fitness/Safety

 **f.** Encyclopedias/Biographies/ Dictionary

---

1. On which icon would you click to find out about the invention of the cotton gin? _____

2. To find out about basic first aid, on which icon would you click? _____

3. On which icon would you click to help you meet other Harry Potter fans? _____

4. You have a report due on comets. On which icon will you click? _____

5. To find out about the life of Abraham Lincoln, which icon will you click? _____

Sentence Comprehension

Directions: Read the sentence carefully and use it to answer the following questions "True" (T) or "False" (F).

> Sandia Mountain rises from the desert floor of New Mexico like a magnificent wave, cresting in a ridge of pine trees and rock.

1. Pine trees grow in the desert. _____

2. The Sandia Mountain was created by an ancient wave that washed over New Mexico. _____

3. There is a desert in New Mexico. _____

4. The Sandia Mountain is described as magnificent. _____

5. The Sandia Mountain is a volcano, rising from the desert floor. _____

Word Study

Directions: Read the information given below and use it to answer the following questions "True" (T) or "False" (F).

Homophones

Words that sound the same, but are spelled differently and have different meanings are called *homophones.* We sometimes think of them as homonyms, but homophone is a more exact description. For example, look at *sight* and *site.* They sound alike, but are spelled differently and mean different things. *Sight* is related to seeing, but *site* means a place, a specific location. Other such pairs are to *complement* (to complete) and *compliment* (to praise someone). A *bazaar* is a open market, where you might find *bizarre* or very strange things. In a church, the *altar*, or central place of worship should not be *altered* or changed without permission. We like *principals* of schools to have good *principles* or standards in which they believe. And we hope the store we go to for *stationery* or writing paper is *stationary* and not moving around. Sometimes there are three homophones as in *rite* (a ritual practice), *right* (to be correct), and *write* (to transcribe letters). A *burro* or donkey left its *borough* or town to find a *burrow* or hole in which to sleep.

And finally, three pairs that cause a lot of trouble among students of English are *theirs* (the possessive) and *there's* (there is), *whose* (possessive) and *who's* (who is), and *its* (the possessive) and *it's* (it is). One way to tell the difference is to remember that no possessive pronoun ever takes an apostrophe!

1. Homophones only come in pairs. _____

2. Homophones are always spelled differently. _____

3. Homophones do not always sound alike. _____

4. Possessive pronouns always take apostrophes. _____

5. A site is a specific place. _____

Paragraph Comprehension

Directions: Read the paragraph below and use it to answer the following questions.

> The mountain is also close to the hearts of the 481 members of the Sandia Pueblo, a 700-
> year-old Native American community. They say that the mountain is sacred. In August,
> 1998, a judge ruled that a big chunk of Sandia's wilderness belongs to the pueblo. But the
> ruling should not be allowed to stand. Nearby nature lovers should not have to give up their
> land.

1. Why did the judge rule that the mountain belongs to the members of the pueblo?

     a. They bought it 700 years ago.

     b. It is part of the wilderness.

     c. Everyone agreed it is theirs.

     d. It is sacred.

2. The nearby nature lovers probably want to

     a. knock the mountain down and build a mall.

     b. sell the mountain.

     c. continue to hike and enjoy the mountain.

     d. have parties on the mountain.

3. According to the paragraph, "a judge ruled." What is another word for *ruled*?

     a. allowed

     b. decided

     c. alleviated

     d. prosecuted

4. What is the ethnic background of people of the Sandia Pueblo?

     a. Mexican

     b. Spanish

     c. Aborigine

     d. Native American

5. The mountain is *close to their hearts* means

     a. they have emotional ties to the mountain.

     b. they live on the mountain.

     c. they will get a lot of money for the mountain.

     d. they often camp in the mountain.

Whole Story Comprehension

Directions: Read the story below and use it to answer the questions on the following page.

The Sandia Pueblo Should Share the Land

Sandia Mountain rises from the desert floor of New Mexico like a magnificent wave, cresting in a ridge of pine trees and rock. It is part of the Cibola National Forest and a favorite getaway place for the nearly 500,000 people who live in Albuquerque (al-buh-kur-kee). They explore its natural wonders on foot, on mountain bikes, and on hang gliders.

The mountain is also close to the hearts of the 481 members of the Sandia Pueblo, a 700-year-old Native American community. They say that the mountain is sacred. In August, 1998, a judge ruled that a big chunk of Sandia's wilderness belongs to the pueblo. But the ruling should not be allowed to stand. Nearby nature lovers should not have to give up their land.

In 1748, when Spain ruled over parts of the western U.S., a Spanish document defined the borders of the pueblo's land. The tribe says it was given control of Sandia's western slope. The U.S. government disagreed.

For years, the pueblo has wanted more control of sacred areas on Sandia. "We should be able to go there anytime we want," says Alex Lujan, governor of the pueblo, which sued the government to regain the land. However, like all Americans, the pueblo members are free to visit the mountain anytime.

In August, 1998, a judge took a close look at the 250-year-old document and agreed with the Native Americans. He ordered the government to return 9,500 acres of the national forest to the Sandia Pueblo. But the readers of the document have differing interpretations of its Spanish wording.

Sandia Mountain's frequent visitors are concerned that they will lose their beloved playground. They say that parcels of land that have been returned to Native Americans are now strictly off limits to others.

Samuel Wellborn, 11, is very concerned. He spends his Saturday mornings hiking the mountain with his family. "The governor of the pueblo says they will let us on the trails, and this will stand for all time, but the thing is, he won't be there forever," says Samuel. He plans to write letters to pueblo officials urging them to keep the trails open to everyone.

Meanwhile, a group of citizens is pushing to have the judge's ruling reversed. The Forest Service, which has controlled the land for 82 years, may challenge it, too.

The 1998 ruling is wrong and should be reversed. It is clear that many groups disagree with the ruling. They believe that it would be a shame to turn stunning Sandia Mountain into forbidden territory for hikers and hang gliders.

Whole Story Comprehension (cont.)

Directions: After you have read the story on the previous page, answer the questions below.

1. If the Sandia Mountain is like a wave, the desert is like a(n)

    a. beach.

    b. ocean.

    c. forest.

    d. lake.

2. Who disagrees with the 1998 verdict of the judge?

    a. the Forest Service

    b. a group of citizens

    c. Samuel Wellborn

    d. all of the above

3. How long ago did Spain give the Sandia Pueblo control of the western slope of the Sandia Mountain?

    a. 750 years ago

    b. 82 years ago

    c. 250 years ago

    d. 700 years ago

4. Why do those who want the trails open not accept the word of the governor of the pueblo?

    a. His word will not be binding when another governor is in power.

    b. He has lied before.

    c. He is saying what hikers want to hear so that the judge will let the pueblos keep the land.

    d. He has written letters to urge the members to close the trails.

5. For what reasons is land considered sacred?

    a. political

    b. sentimental

    c. religious

    d. scientific

6. Who is Lujan?

    a. the judge

    b. the governor of Albuquerque

    c. the governor of the pueblo

    d. an avid hiker

7. Choose the statement that is not true.

    a. The pueblos believe the judge made the correct decision in giving them control of the Sandia Mountain.

    b. Samuel Wellborn wants the town to build a permanent campground on the Sandia Mountain.

    c. The 1748 document is in Spanish because Spain ruled what is now New Mexico.

    d. The judge's 1998 ruling is based on an interpretation of the 1748 Spanish document.

8. The argument described in this article is a legal battle over

    a. constitutional rights.

    b. political beliefs.

    c. money.

    d. land.

Enrichment

Directions: Read the information below and use it to answer the following questions.

Noun Clauses

In English grammar, there are two types of clauses—main clauses and subordinate (or dependent) clauses. A main clause is a complete sentence that can stand by itself, but dependent clauses cannot. They must lean or depend on a main clause. Clauses, even dependent clauses, must always have a subject and a predicate.

One type of dependent clause used in the article of this lesson is the *noun clause*.

A *noun clause* is a dependent clause that functions like a noun. In other words, wherever a noun can be used in a sentence, a noun clause could be used instead. One good way of testing to see if a group of words is a noun clause is to try to replace the whole clause with the pronoun something or someone.

Noun clauses are introduced by such words as *whose, which, whatever, who, whoever, whomever,* and *that*. These are all relative adjectives. Or they can be introduced by words such as *where, when, how, what, that, when,* and *why*. These are all relative adverbs.

Nouns can be used as subjects of sentences; so can noun clauses. Compare: John will have a lot of work to do. Whoever wins the election will have a lot of work to do. (Someone will have a lot of work to do.)

A noun can be used as a predicate nominative after forms of the linking verb to be; so can a noun clause. This is John's job. This is what John will do. (This is something.)

A noun can be used as a direct object of the verb; so can a noun clause. John knows the score. John knows what the score is. (John knows something.)

A noun can be used as the object of a proposition; so can a noun clause. John knew the contents of his speech. John knew the contents of what he had just said. (John knew the contents of something.)

Why is it important to know about noun clauses? When reading, if we can tell how the noun clause relates to the main clause, we are better able to understand the main point of the sentence. To do this, it is important to be able to identify the main verb or predicate of the sentence. When writing, we can improve our sentence structure and avoid tangled sentences and other mistakes.

Carefully read these sentences. Mark the sentences that have noun clauses in them as "Yes" (Y) and those that do not as "No" (N).

1. Many groups disagree with what the judge has ruled. _____
2. But the readers of the document have different interpretations of the Spanish wording. _____
3. Samuel Wellborn, 11, is very concerned with what has happened. _____
4. They believe that it would be a shame to turn stunning Sandia Mountain into forbidden territory for hikers and hang gliders. _____
5. They say that the mountain is sacred. _____
6. Nature lovers should not have to give up their land. _____
7. That the U.S. government disagrees with the pueblo leaders is evident. _____
8. Who will be able to use Sandia Mountain is a concern of the people who visit it frequently. _____
9. They say that parcels of land are now off limits. _____
10. The pueblo members are free to visit the mountain anytime. _____

Graphic Development

Directions: Below are listed events found in the article. They are not in chronological order. Use the information in the article to match these events with the numbers on the time line. Write the correct number next to each event.

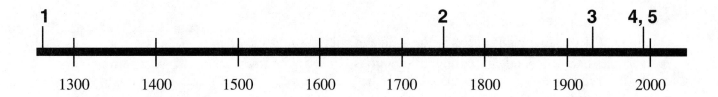

a. _____ date of Spanish document that gave Sandia Pueblo control of Sandia Mountain

b. _____ judge orders 9,500 acres of National Forest returned to Sandia Pueblo

c. _____ the beginning of the Sandia Pueblo

d. _____ a group of citizens try to reverse the judge's ruling

e. _____ National Forest Service first controls Sandia Mountain

Sentence Comprehension

Directions: Read the sentence carefully and use it to answer the following questions "True" (T) or "False" (F).

> Under the Indian constitution, the government must provide food, shelter, schooling, and medical care for the children of tribal people, a promise not always kept.

1. Children of the tribe have a right to be cared for by the government. _____
2. The Indian constitution protects the tribes. _____
3. The government has been true to its word and provides education, food, shelter, and medical care to the children of the tribe. _____
4. According to the Indian constitution, the government must provide an education to every member of the tribe. _____
5. We can be certain from the sentence above that the tribal people referred to are Native American Indians. _____

Word Study

Directions: Read the information given below. If the two words are close in meaning, answer "Yes" (Y) and if they are not close in meaning, answer "No" (N).

> When authors write, they sometimes have a wide choice of words from which to choose. There are dictionaries of synonyms to which they can turn. Some word processors even have a thesaurus, a kind of synonym list, that the writer can use. But it is important to remember that the synonyms for a particular word do not mean exactly the same thing.
>
> In this article, the author tells about a tribal group, the Korku, which is being asked to move out of a Bengal tiger reserve. He writes, "The Korku's plight is reflected across India." "Plight" means a situation from which one can get out of only with great difficulty. But "plight" also suggests an unfortunate, trying, or unhappy situation.
>
> Other words that the author might have used are "predicament" and "dilemma." Both these words suggest that the Korku have a lack of freedom to do what they wish or that they cannot find a way out of their problem. All solutions are unsatisfactory.
>
> Although there are other synonyms listed for plight, the author could not use them because they do not reflect the exact meaning. A quandary means that the problem is so bad that the Korku have lost sight of all possible choices. This is not true of their situation. Other words such as scrape, fix, or jam, which are closer to slang, usually refer to a problem caused by an individual's own misbehavior. The Korku did not cause their own problem.
>
> It is important to look up the meanings of synonyms before they are used.

1. dilemma and predicament _____
2. denote and connote _____
3. scrape and plight _____
4. plight and predicament _____
5. thesaurus and dictionary of synonyms _____

Paragraph Comprehension

Directions: Read the paragraph below and use it to answer the following questions.

For the Korku, the laws are a threat to their very survival. Once nomadic, the Korku were forced to live in settlements in the nineteeth century when Britain ruled India. They became farmers, but depended on the forest for fruit, nuts, roots, and firewood.

1. The tribal name of the nomadic group is the

    a. Korku.

    b. British.

    c. Nomads.

    d. Farmers.

2. The Korku were once nomadic. *Nomadic* means that

    a. they prefer to live in permanent settlements.

    b. the tribe moves frequently to obtain a good food supply.

    c. they eat only fruit.

    d. they fight for survival.

3. What country is home to the Korku?

    a. India

    b. Britain

    c. They travel to no one particular country.

    d. Korkia

4. Now that the Korku must remain in settlements, the tribe

    a. is a hunting community.

    b. is nomadic.

    c. mainly hunts and gathers.

    d. is a farming community.

5. Who forced the Korku to give up their nomadic lifestyle?

    a. the leader of the tribe

    b. the priests of the Korku

    c. the rulers of India

    d. the British government

Whole Story Comprehension

Directions: Read the story below and use it to answer the questions on the following page.

Tragedy in the Jungle

Within the lush Melghat rain forest in central India lives a colony of magnificent but endangered beasts, 70 bengal tigers. They are the last of hundreds that roamed the region less that 100 years ago. The Indian government has passed laws to protect the tigers. But there's a big problem: the laws threaten human lives.

The tigers of the Melghat Tiger Reserve share the area with the Korku, a tribe of forest dwellers. To protect the tigers, the government has barred the Korku from using the Melghat. The government wants to move 11 Korku villages out to the reserve. An additional 39 villages, which are on the fringes, will be allowed to remain. But villagers may no longer gather firewood or food or graze cattle in the reserve.

For the Korku, the laws are a threat to their very survival. Once nomadic, the Korku were forced to live in settlements in the 19th century when Britain ruled India. They became farmers, but depended on the forest for fruit, nuts, roots, and firewood.

It is a difficult way of life. Since 1993, hundreds of Korku children have died because they did not have enough food. Without the reserves' resources, even more would perish.

"The officials keep talking about saving the tiger. Don't they care about people?" asks Sonaji Dhande, a farmer. "If we leave the forest, our Korku tradition will vanish."

The Korku's plight is reflected across India. At least eight million people live in or around India's 23 tiger reserves. The reserves are home to 3,000 tigers that have managed to survive illegal hunting and the destruction of their habitat. Now, conservation laws are making it hard for humans and tigers to live together.

In January, 1997, the government decided to stop forcing villagers to move out of the reserve. It wants them to move voluntarily. Under the Indian constitution, the government must provide food, shelter, schooling, and medical care for the children of tribal people, a promise not always kept.

Conservationists admit they do not know what to do with the villagers. "There is so much hunger outside the reserves. Where do we settle them?" asks P. K. Sen, director of Project Tiger, India's program to save tigers.

The villagers of the Melghat insist that they are not a threat to the great cats that have been their neighbors for so many years. "We have no quarrel with the tiger," says Onkar Shikari, an elderly Korku. "We respect one another."

Whole Story Comprehension (cont.)

Directions: After you have read the story on the previous page, answer the questions below.

1. In addition to farming, on what do the Korku depend for food?

    a. the government

    b. the British

    c. the forest

    d. hunting

2. The 11 Korku villages that are in the Melghat must share the area with

    a. 39 other villages.

    b. grazing cattle.

    c. the tiger reserve.

    d. all of the above

3. The laws that help protect the bengal tiger

    a. have forbidden the Korku to use the forest.

    b. also endanger the lives of the Korku.

    c. are threatening the tradition and culture of the Korku.

    d. all of the above

4. What is the name of India's program to save the Bengal tiger?

    a. Melghat Tiger Reserve

    b. Sanaji Dhande

    c. Project Tiger

    d. all of the above

5. Why does the government forbid the Korku to use the forest?

    a. The Korku hunt tigers.

    b. The Korku will eat all of the tigers' food.

    c. The cattle disturb the tigers.

    d. It wants to protect the tigers' habitat.

6. Choose the statement that is true.

    a. Korku children have all died from starvation.

    b. The government has kept its promise to support the children of the tribe.

    c. The villagers continue to be forced to relocate.

    d. The Melghat Reserve is the only tiger reserve in India.

7. Which of the following do we know to be true about Project Tiger?

    a. There are 23 tiger reserves in India.

    b. Project Tiger protects 1,000 tigers.

    c. Project Tiger threatens the welfare of eight million villagers.

    d. all of the above

8. Onkar Shikari believes that the answer to the problem is

    a. to let the Korku and the tigers share the forest.

    b. to cancel Project Tiger.

    c. to force the government to keep its promises.

    d. to move the villagers to better farmland.

Enrichment

Directions: Read the information below and use it answer the following questions.

Similes

Years ago more people lived closer to nature, like the Korku live in the forest today. At that time, a number of **similes** were first used to compare the qualities of a person to those of an animal, bird, or insect. These expressions remain in our language today. A *simile* is a comparison using like or as. These figures of speech are used like adjectives or adverbs. They describe a person with a colorful, and often, visual phrase. Some of them are so commonly used that we forget that they were once a fresh and unusual way of describing a person.

Here are a few examples:

a. blind as bat   d. strong as an ox   g. quiet as a mouse

b. sick as a dog   e. eager as a beaver   h. busy as a bee

c. eyes like a hawk   f. drinks like a fish   i. like a bull in a china shop

There are many other expressions that use animals, birds, or insects to describe situations.

j. He is running around like a chicken with his head cut off.

k. He has bats in his belfry.

l. He had more than the lion's share.

m. We made him eat crow.

n. We sent him on a wild goose chase.

o. It was raining cats and dogs.

p. The robber flew the coop.

q. He was always buying a pig in a poke.

r. During the last year of their second term, American presidents are considered lame ducks.

s. The boy was a bad egg from the beginning.

t. That party was more fun than a barrel of monkeys.

u. Thomas Edison had a bee in his bonnet about an electric light bulb.

v. The football team always brought home the bacon.

Choose one of the lettered items above to match each situation or definition below.

1. All night I was vomiting. _____

2. She sees everything and never misses a thing. _____

3. He consumes a lot of liquid, especially alcohol. _____

4. He is very clumsy and breaks everything. _____

5. We made him apologize. _____

6. to win the prize _____

7. not able to see _____

8. to escape _____

9. to have a fixed idea about doing something _____

10. not being able to concentrate on doing one thing _____

Graphic Development

Directions: Look carefully at the picture and write if the statements are "True" (T) or "False" (F).

1. The Korku have a primitive lifestyle. _____

2. The woman is sitting by the fire to keep warm in the cold climate of India. _____

3. The shelter in the background indicates that people live in a warm climate. _____

4. The Korku appear to live in family groups. _____

5. Based on the information in the article and the picture, the Korku woman is cooking tiger. _____

Sentence Comprehension

Directions: Read the sentence carefully and use it to answer the following questions "True" (T) or "False" (F).

In early 1998, Brazil's government confirmed what environmentalists have feared: the 1990s were a terrible decade for the rain forest.

---

1. Environmentalists were concerned about the loss of forest land prior to 1998. _____

2. The rain forest in Brazil is in danger of being destroyed. _____

3. A report was released by Brazil's governments in 1998. _____

4. The 1990s were terrible for the rain forest because tourism was down in Brazil. _____

5. A decade is 10 years. _____

Word Study

Directions: Read the information given below and use it to answer the following questions "True" (T) or "False" (F).

Satellite

Today, we think nothing of man-made space *satellites* circling the earth or another heavenly body. But a *satellite* can also be a natural object in space that orbits a celestial body of a larger size. The moon is a *satellite* of Earth. The earth is a *satellite* of the sun.

Satellite also has a less heavenly meaning. A company or a country, which is dependent upon a larger organization, is also a *satellite* of that organization. For example, Puerto Rico is a satellite of the United States. Russia once had many *satellite* countries.

An individual who is devoted to someone more powerful could be called a *satellite*. More often, we call that kind of person a disciple or a follower. But we don't describe *satellites* in the sky this way.

---

1. Satellites are found only in the heavens. _____

2. A synonym for satellite is disciple. _____

3. We would usually call the moon a disciple of the earth. _____

4. *To orbit* means the same as to circle. _____

5. Satellites are never natural objects. _____

Paragraph Comprehension

Directions: Read the information given below and use it to answer the following questions.

Space satellites regularly take pictures of the Amazon. The information released by Brazil was based on these pictures. Deforestation slowed down in 1995 and 1997. But that's not necessarily because people were protecting the forest. It's because heavy rainfall made it harder to burn trees. "These numbers are no reason to celebrate," admits Brazil's Environment Minister, Gustavo Krause.

---

1. The deforestation of the rain forest lowered. What does this tell us?

    a. People are beginning to protect against losing the rain forest.

    b. The heavy rainfall helped more trees to grow.

    c. The problem is over.

    d. Rainfall made it difficult to burn the trees.

2. How can we tell how much of the rain forest is lost each year?

    a. Permits are needed to burn trees.

    b. Gustavo Krause measures the forest yearly.

    c. Photos from space show deforestation.

    d. Loggers must document what they cut.

3. What position does Gustavo Krause hold in Brazil's government?

    a. Head of the Environment Protection Agency

    b. Environment Czar

    c. Forest Minister

    d. Environment Minister

4. Where is the Brazilian rain forest found?

    a. Amazon

    b. satellite

    c. deforestation

    d. New York

5. What does Gustavo Krause learn from the rain forest photos taken by the space satellites?

    a. the number of square miles lost in the Amazon rain forest

    b. that the protection of the rain forest is making a difference

    c. the number of trees cut down

    d. the number of farmers living in the rain forest

Whole Story Comprehension

Directions: Read the story below and use it to answer the questions on the following page.

Amazon Alert!

The lush Amazon rain forest stretches about 2.7 million square miles. Brightly colored parrots, swift jaguars, and fierce piranhas make their home in the tropical forest and its many rivers. Monkeys swing among high branches and vines. The Amazon holds one-fifth of the planet's freshwater supply and the world's widest variety of life.

For decades, this wildlife wonderland has been shrinking as farmers and others clear the land. In early 1998, Brazil's government confirmed what environmentalists have feared: the 1990s were a terrible decade for the rain forest. The destruction of the forest in Brazil reached record levels in 1995. In that year alone, 11,200 square miles were burned or cleared. That's nearly twice what was lost in 1994. Over all, one-eighth of the giant rain forest has been destroyed.

The bad news from Brazil was followed by a ray of hope. Brazil promised to do a better job enforcing laws that protect its natural treasure.

Loggers, miners, and farmers from Brazil and nearby countries have been rapidly moving into the Amazon since the 1960s. Some cut down trees for wood and paper. Others simply burn the forest to clear the land. Construction of roads and airplane runways has also damaged the region. The loss of trees is deforestation.

Space satellites regularly take pictures of the Amazon. The information released by Brazil was based on these pictures. Deforestation slowed down in 1995 and 1997. But that's not necessarily because people were protecting the forest. It's because heavy rainfall made it harder to burn trees. "These numbers are no reason to celebrate," admits Brazil's Environment Minister, Gustavo Krause.

Stephan Schwartzman of the Environmental Defense Fund calls the pace of destruction "alarming." He and other scientists are worried that they will run out of time to study the plants and animals of the rich forest. "The great tragedy is how much isn't known," he says.

To slow down deforestation, Brazil decided to get tougher on people who abuse the Amazon. In 1996, Brazil placed limits on clearing land in the region. But officials did not always enforce the laws. Now those who damage the rain forest will be punished with big fines and ordered to repair the damage. "This can make a big difference," says Schwartzman. "There is hope."

Whole Story Comprehension (cont.)

Directions: After you have read the story on the previous page, answer the questions below.

1. *Deforestation* means
    a. slash and burn.
    b. the loss of trees.
    c. great tragedy.
    d. enforcing forest protection laws.

2. When did the deforestation of the rain forest begin?
    a. 1990
    b. 1960
    c. 1994
    d. 2.7 million years ago

3. Why do farmers burn the rain forest?
    a. to clear the land
    b. to make paper
    c. to created space for runways
    d. all of the above

4. What does Stephan Schwartzman mean by "The greatest tragedy is how much isn't known"?
    a. After the rain forest is destroyed, the plants and animals are lost forever.
    b. Scientists haven't studied all the plants and animals of the forest.
    c. All the lost plants and animals were potentially valuable sources of information.
    d. All of the statements above are valid explanations of the quote.

5. Which of the following creatures of the Amazon makes its home in the Amazon River?
    a. jaguars
    b. piranha
    c. monkeys
    d. parrots

6. How much of the rain forest has been lost?
    a. 11,200 square miles
    b. 1/8
    c. 1/5
    d. 80%

7. What does Brazil plan to do to protect the rain forest?
    a. create new laws
    b. enforce laws they already have
    c. plant trees
    d. ban farming

8. The Amazon is called Brazil's
    a. wildlife wonderland.
    b. environmental disaster.
    c. natural treasure.
    d. a and c

Enrichment

Directions: Read the information given below and use it to answer the following questions "True" (T) or "False" (F).

We can break the word *deforestation* into several parts. The core of this word is *forest*. When we add "-ation", we add the idea that we are going to create a forest.

But when we place the prefix "de-" in front of the word, we make the word negative. We are now talking about the opposite of putting a forest on a piece of land. We are talking about removing a forest from an area.

The meaning of "de-" in *deforestation* is to remove. If someone is asked by a government to leave a country, that person is *deported*. To *delouse* someone is to remove lice from that person. A king could be *dethroned*, or removed from his throne. The Revolutionary War was fought so that America would no longer be a colony of England. America became *de-colonized*. To *declassify* a document is to remove it from a group of papers that the government needs to keep secret.

Another meaning of "de-" is to reduce. If the dollar is *devalued*, it is worth less than it was before. If a building is *defaced*, it is made less beautiful. The form of an object could be *deformed*, or made less perfect.

A third meaning of "de-" is to do the opposite. If we *de-emphasize* a topic, we make it less important. To *deactivate* a bomb is to make it non-active so it will not explode.

And finally, "de-" can mean to get off a specific thing. To *detrain* means to get off the train. To *deplane* is to get off the plane.

It is important to remember that the "de-" at the beginning of some words does not always represent a prefix. Nor are all words that begin with "de-" negative. Words such as *delight*, *decorate, degree, delicatessen, depot, dentist,* or *dense* all fall into this last category.

And the word *denude* actually means to make something more nude, to strip it of all covering. The "de-" intensifies the meaning. For example, the land was *denuded* by erosion.

_____ 1. Delight means that light is removed.

_____ 2. Deforestation means that a forest has been removed.

_____ 3. When a train is derailed, it has gotten off its tracks.

_____ 4. When a balloon is deflated, air has been removed from it.

_____ 5. If salinization means to fill water with salt, desalinization means to remove salt from water.

_____ 6. If to attach means to connect, to detach means to separate.

_____ 7. To reduce and to remove mean the same thing.

Graphic Development

Directions: Study the bar graph below and write if the statements are "True" (T) or "False" (F).

Yearly Rain Forest Loss

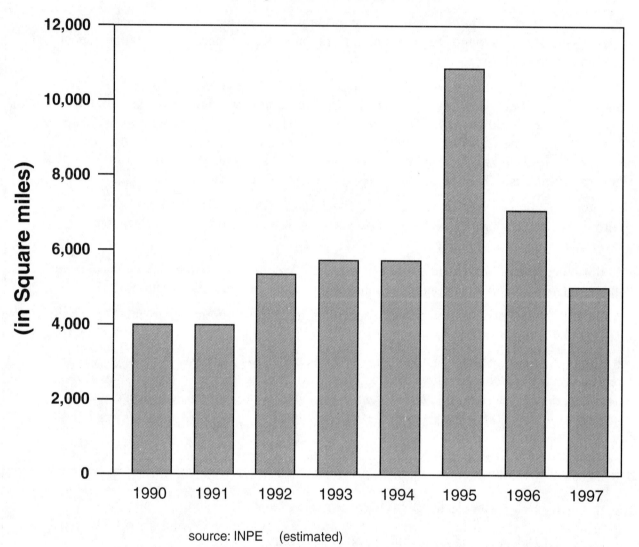

source: INPE   (estimated)

1. In 1990 and 1991, there was a combined loss of 4,000 square miles of rain forest. _____

2. The first year to show a decrease in rain forest destruction is 1997. _____

3. The unit of measure for yearly loss is square miles. _____

4. The same amount of rain forest loss is shown in 1992 and 1993. _____

5. From 1990 to 1994, over 30,000 square miles of rain forest were lost. _____

Sentence Comprehension

Directions: Read the sentence carefully and use it to answer the following questions "True" (T) or "False" (F).

> Whenever something is burned, such as fuel in a car, coal to make electric power, or trees to clear land for farming, pollution goes into the air.

1. Cars burn fuel. _____
2. Coal is burned to make electric power. _____
3. Some farmers burn trees. _____
4. Burning fuel causes pollution. _____
5. Pollution is bad for the air. _____

Word Study

Directions: Read the information given below and use it to answer the following questions "True" (T) or "False" (F).

> **Greenhouse**
>
> *Greenhouse effect* is a term frequently included in any discussion of global warming. To understand its meaning, we need to know what a *greenhouse* is. *Greenhouses* are used to grow and protect tender plants. To make a *greenhouse*, we need to construct a frame on which can be placed translucent or cloudy glass or plastic through which the sun can shine. The heat of the sun can be absorbed by the plants and dirt or it can be reflected back to the covering. But because the glass is translucent, the heat waves cannot pass back through the covering to the outside. Thus, the inside of a *greenhouse* is warmer than the temperature outside.
>
> Approximately one-sixth of the energy that comes from the sun passes through the atmosphere to the earth and heats the earth. When that heat is reflected back to the atmosphere, it does not pass through because the atmosphere is like the translucent windows of a *greenhouse*. Some scientists think that the more carbon dioxide there is in the atmosphere, the more heat will be trapped beneath the atmosphere. The earth then becomes warmer. This increased warming is called the *greenhouse* effect.
>
> Another name for a *greenhouse* is a conservatory, because a *greenhouse* conserves whatever is inside. Schools for artists are called conservatories. A music conservatory "grows" and protects young musicians.

1. *Greenhouses* are made of a frame and clear glass. _____
2. All heat from the sun is reflected back to the covering of the *greenhouse*. _____
3. The temperatures inside and outside of a *greenhouse* are different. _____
4. The atmosphere is like the covering of a *greenhouse*._____
5. To become a musician, one would go to a music *greenhouse*. _____

Paragraph Comprehension

Directions: Read the paragraph below and use it to answer the following questions.

Whenever something is burned, fuel in a car, coal to make electric power, or trees to clear land for farming, pollution goes into the air. Part of pollution is carbon dioxide gas. When carbon dioxide gets into the atmosphere, it prevents the heat from the sun from escaping from the earth. The heat is needed to keep the earth warm. However, as pollution increases, so does the amount of carbon dioxide. More heat is trapped, and the earth gets warmer. This is sometimes called the "greenhouse effect." The trapped warm air makes the earth much like a very hot greenhouse. A warmer earth could cause the climate to change.

1. Which activity is absolutely not going to contribute to air pollution?

   a. turning on an electric light

   b. trapping the heat of the sun with solar panels

   c. driving to a friend's house

   d. roasting marshmallows over an open campfire

2. Carbon dioxide is a natural gas. Humans exhale it, and it is naturally present in the atmosphere. What is the problem with carbon dioxide as described in this paragraph?

   a. There is too much carbon dioxide.

   b. The sun is getting hotter.

   c. Carbon dioxide generates heat.

   d. none of the above

3. As pollution increases,

   a. more heat is trapped.

   b. more carbon dioxide will be found in the atmosphere.

   c. the earth will get warmer.

   d. all of the above

4. If the earth is like a greenhouse, the carbon dioxide is like

   a. the plants that grow inside.

   b. the sun that heats it.

   c. the cover on the greenhouse that keeps in the heat.

   d. the farmer who grows plants.

5. If an increase in pollution means more heat is trapped, a decrease means

   a. the earth will freeze.

   b. less heat is trapped.

   c. another ice age will come.

   d. the greenhouse effect will occur.

Whole Story Comprehension

Directions: Read the story below and use it to answer the questions on the following page.

Global Warming

Many scientists believe that the earth is slowly getting warmer. Over the past hundred years, the temperature of the earth has increased by about one degree Fahrenheit. Is this cause for alarm? Is the earth's climate changing? If the earth is getting warmer, what do some scientists say is the cause?

Whenever something is burned, fuel in a car, coal to make electric power, or trees to clear land for farming, pollution goes into the air. Part of pollution is carbon dioxide gas. When carbon dioxide gets into the atmosphere, it prevents the heat from the sun from escaping from the earth. The heat is needed to keep the earth warm. However, as pollution increases, so does the amount of carbon dioxide. More heat is trapped, and the earth gets warmer. This is sometimes called the "greenhouse effect." The trapped warm air makes the earth much like a greenhouse. A warmer earth could cause the climate to change.

Many scientists and environmentalists believe that the only way to stop global warming is to cut down on carbon dioxide pollution. To reach such a goal, people throughout the world would have to cooperate and look for new ways to reduce pollution.

Whole Story Comprehension *(cont.)*

Directions: After you have read the story on the previous page, answer the questions below.

1. The "greenhouse effect" causes

   a. more carbon dioxide in the atmosphere.

   b. larger plants and trees.

   c. global warming.

   d. pollution.

2. The earth's temperature has gone up one degree Fahrenheit

   a. every year since the invention of the automobile.

   b. in the past hundred years.

   c. every one hundred years.

   d. since the creation of carbon dioxide.

3. What do people do that adds to pollution?

   a. use carpools

   b. use public transportation

   c. burn garbage

   d. cut down trees

4. What is the major source of air pollution?

   a. a campfire

   b. an airplane

   c. fires that clear the rainforest

   d. carbon dioxide

5. "Global warming"

   a. means the earth is getting warmer.

   b. is the same as the sun getting hotter.

   c. is the same as pollution.

   d. is the same as trapped heat.

6. If the cause is the "greenhouse effect," what is the effect?

   a. more carbon dioxide

   b. possibly a change in the earth's climate

   c. a reduction in pollution

   d. none of the above

7. A person who works to protect the air, water, animals, plants, and natural resources from the effects of pollution is called a/an

   a. scientist.

   b. environmentalist.

   c. geologist.

   d. biologist.

8. What is needed for an environment in which humans can live?

   a. the air we breathe

   b. the land which supplies us food

   c. the water we drink

   d. all of the above

Enrichment

Directions: Read the information below and use it to match the objects with the words.

Using specific adjectives that suggest the texture of an object described or that indicate how something feels helps the writer share the experience being described.

On the right is a list of objects. How would you expect these objects to feel? On the left is a list of specific words that describe various textures. Match the objects with the words.

Words

1. bumpy _____

2. fluffy _____

3. furry _____

4. jagged _____

5. prickly _____

6. rough _____

7. smooth _____

8. slippery _____

9. sharp _____

10. sticky _____

Objects

a. honey on a piece of toast

b. the inside of a pair of gloves lined with sheep's skin

c. the edge of a piece of broken, rusty metal

d. a cactus

e. a wet bar of soap

f. the side surface of a soda can

g. feathers in a pillow

h. the bark of a tree

i. riding over holes in a roadway

j. the cutting edge of a knife

Graphic Development

Directions: Look carefully at the two cartoons and tell if the statements below are "True" (T) or "False" (F).

1. The viewer needs to understand what global warming means in order to understand both cartoons. _____

2. The boy in Cartoon A wants his father to tell about global warming again because he wonders where the predicted warm weather is. _____

3. We can tell that the father in Cartoon A is angry about his son's question. _____

4. The speaker in Cartoon B knows what global warming means. _____

5. The creator of Cartoon B is saying that global warming is a myth, a story that cannot be believed. _____

Sentence Comprehension

Directions: Read the sentence carefully and use it to answer the following questions "True" (T) or "False" (F).

> With help from the federal government, researchers are trying to develop one shot that would protect against all 10 diseases.

1. The federal government is funding research in the field of immunization. _____

2. There is presently only one shot needed to administer vaccines for 10 childhood diseases. _____

3. A researcher can work for the government. _____

4. The federal government is in favor of having one shot instead of 10. _____

5. The government believes childhood diseases are causes for concern. _____

Word Study

Directions: Read the information given below and use it to answer the following questions "True" (T) or "False" (F).

> **Immune**
>
> Whenever we go to a doctor to get a shot to protect us from getting a disease, we receive an *immunization*. We all have an *immune* system that produces antibodies that protect us from diseases. But our *immune* systems do not protect us from all diseases. A scientist, or an *immunologist*, studies *immunology* and tries to discover the causes of diseases and how to improve *immunity*.
>
> *Immunity* also has a non-medical meaning. It means to be free from, or protected against, something burdensome or disagreeable or painful. For instance, in exchange for cooperating with the police, an individual could be *immune* from prosecution in a court of law. In non-scientific areas, exemption is a synonym for *immunity*, but *immunity* suggests that an individual is especially favored or privileged by law or birth. For instance, the king granted the nobles *immunity* from taxation.

1. If we received a shot to prevent us from getting chicken pox, we would be *immunized* against that disease. _____

2. A scientist who studies the *immune* system is an exemptionist. _____

3. An individual could be *immune* from punishment. _____

4. When we ask a doctor for an exemption from measles, he would know what we mean. _____

5. We could be exempt from taking an exam, but not *immune* from it. _____

Paragraph Comprehension

Directions: Read the paragraph below and use it to answer the following questions.

Here's a shot of good news. More American babies than ever before are protected against 10 childhood diseases. In 1992, only 55% of children under age two had the immunizations or shots they needed. In 1996, about 75% of kids under two were immunized.

1. The statistics are

    a. worldwide.

    b. state by state.

    c. for the United States.

    d. none of the above

2. Another word used for immunization is

    a. shot.

    b. protection.

    c. immunized.

    d. all of the above

3. Which statement about the paragraph is not true?

    a. Two different years are compared.

    b. Two different percentages are compared.

    c. Two different age groups are compared.

    d. There was an increase of almost 20% in the number of children immunized from 1992 to 1996.

4. With immunizations on the rise, childhood diseases would most likely

    a. decrease.

    b. increase.

    c. stay the same.

    d. be hard to determine.

5. In 1996, the study was conducted on children

    a. living in the United States in 1993.

    b. living in the United States in 1994.

    c. under the age of two.

    d. over the age of two.

Whole Story Comprehension

Directions: Read the story below and use it to answer the questions on the following page.

A Healthy Rise in Vaccinations

Here's a shot of good news. More American babies than ever before are protected against 10 childhood diseases. In 1992, only 55% of children under age two had the immunizations or shots they needed. In 1996, about 75% of kids under two were immunized.

"Childhood infectious diseases are at an all-time low," said Secretary of Health and Human Services, Donna Shalala, who announced the statistics.

Raising immunization rates has long been a goal of President Bill Clinton. He introduced a plan in 1994 to provide cheaper—sometimes free—shots, more places where kids can get immunized, and more information for parents about what shots children need.

Shalala pointed out that protection from measles, chicken pox, mumps, and other diseases is not just for babies. "Booster shots are like refilling the gas tank, making sure your immune system is able to run," she said.

With help from the federal government, researchers are trying to develop one shot that would protect against all 10 diseases. That would mean fewer "ouches" at the doctor's office.

Whole Story Comprehension *(cont.)*

Directions: After you have read the story on the previous page, answer the questions below.

1. What wording suggests that immunizations have been good for American children?

    a. "cheaper—sometimes free—shots"

    b. "a shot of good news"

    c. "75% of kids under two were immunized."

    d. "Childhood infectious diseases are at an all-time low."

2. What is the best synonym for vaccination?

    a. infectious disease

    b. immune system

    c. immature

    d. shot

3. "Booster shots are like refilling the gas tank" is a

    a. simile.

    b. metaphor.

    c. synonym.

    d. antonym.

4. In the 1990s, the number of children receiving immunization seems to be

    a. increasing.

    b. decreasing.

    c. holding steady.

    d. at an all time low.

5. Who is the expert quoted in the article?

    a. Bill Clinton

    b. The federal government

    c. Dr. Donna Shalala

    d. The Secretary of State

6. What has the government done to make sure that parents who want their children immunized are able to have this done?

    a. provide more information to parents

    b. administer low cost and free vaccines

    c. open more places to get shots

    d. all of the above

7. Some immunizations are given again when a child is older. What are these called?

    a. a refill

    b. free shots

    c. protection

    d. booster shots

8. Against what do immunizations usually protect children?

    a. all childhood diseases

    b. the 10 childhood infectious diseases

    c. mumps, measles, and chickenpox

    d. colds

Enrichment

Directions: Read the information below and use it to find a proverb in the alphabetized list that warns about a situation in the numbered items.

Proverbs

The writer begins this article with "Here's a shot of good news." The writer is playing with the word *shot*. We get shots to prevent us from catching diseases, but we can also "get a shot of good news." Actually, the idiom is "a shot in the arm." A shot in the arm is something inspiring or encouraging. For example, we were ready to quit, but the coach's talk was a shot in the arm. The coach's talk inspired us.

In an idiom, a new meaning is given to a group of words that already has its own meaning. One type of idiom is a proverb. A *proverb* is a sentence or a phrase which briefly and memorably states some recognized truth about practical life. It usually has been passed down orally from generation to generation.

An example of a proverb is, "Eat an apple a day and keep the doctor away." Many proverbs warn us. The Chinese say, "Beware of what you wish for; you might get it."

Proverbs

   a. Don't count your chickens before they hatch.
   b. Don't put all your eggs in one basket.
   c. Never judge a book by its cover.
   d. You can lead a horse to water, but you can't make it drink.
   e. One swallow does not a summer make.
   f. When the cat is away, the mice will play.
   g. People who live in glass houses should not throw stones.
   h. Too many cooks spoil the broth.
   i. Half a loaf is better than none.
   j. A bird in the hand is worth two in the bush.

Situations

_____   1. You were very excited when you got a big box for your birthday, but you were disappointed to discover that it contained only pair of socks.

_____   2. Your brother says that he will only apply to one college and not several.

_____   3. Three different people made different arrangements for the class party and now there is total confusion.

_____   4. John does not always tell the truth, but he is always accusing others of lying.

_____   5. Whenever the teacher is out of the room, the students misbehave.

_____   6. Students can be forced to go to school, but that does not mean they will learn.

_____   7. Just because you got one good grade in math, does not mean that all the rest of your grades are going to be good.

_____   8. It is better to have an actual dollar than to have a promise of ten dollars.

_____   9. Mary didn't accept one piece of pizza because she wanted a whole pie, but she ended up with none at all.

_____   10. The class looked forward to a picnic, but it rained.

Graphic Development

Directions: Study the map printed below and use the information in the article to tell if the statements are "True" (T) or "False" (F).

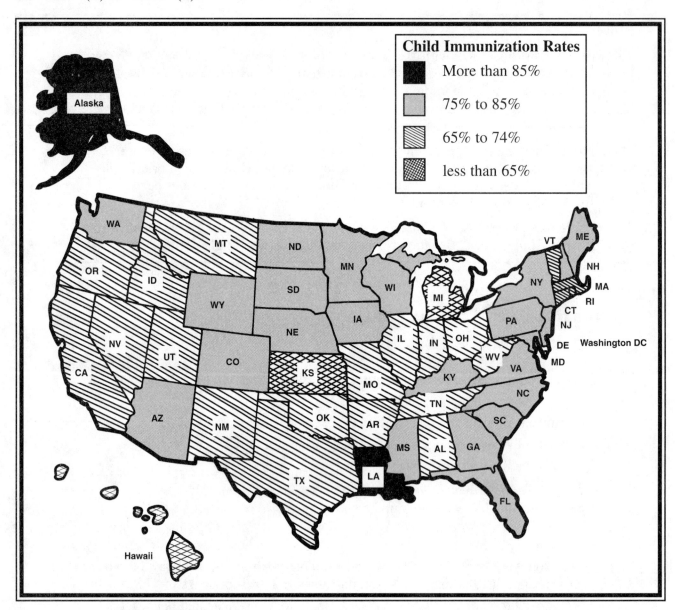

1. The percentage of children immunized on the East Coast is at least 85%. _____

2. The states where a child is least likely to have been immunized are Kansas, Michigan, and Hawaii. _____

3. Vermont may have a 100% immunization rate. _____

4. A child is more likely to have been immunized in California than in Florida. _____

5. At least 65% of all children in each state are immunized. _____

Sentence Comprehension

Directions: Read the sentence carefully and use it to answer the following questions "True" (T) or "False" (F).

In a speech to the Child Labor Coalition, U.S. Secretary of Labor Robert Reich expressed gratitude for the organization's work to end abuse of child labor: "You turned up the heat, and you got results."

---

1. Robert Reich works for the Child Labor Coalition. _____

2. The Secretary of Labor believes that abusing working children is wrong. _____

3. The Child Labor Coalition supports all businesses that utilize child labor. _____

4. *You turned up the heat* means they burned down businesses that abuse working children. _____

5. The abuse of child labor has now ended worldwide. _____

Word Study

Directions: Read the information given below and use it to answer the following questions "True" (T) or "False" (F).

Coalition

Coalition is made up of two parts. The first part means together like the *co-* in *cooperate*. The second part, *-alition*, means "to grow." Thus, *coalition* means to grow together, to unite separate parts or individuals into a whole. Usually these individuals are joined together for a common cause. The individuals merge and blend so well because they have a natural *affinity* or attraction. That *affinity* is caused by a common interest. The Child Labor *Coalition* is an organization made up of a group of people and organizations that are interested in ending the abuse of child labor. They are all interested in improving the conditions of children who work.

---

1. *Co-* means to grow. _____

2. *Affinity* means the same as attraction. _____

3. A *coalition* is interested only in improving conditions for working children. _____

4. A *coalition* could be formed to improve school lunches. _____

5. A *coalition* could be made up of only one person. _____

Paragraph Comprehension

Directions: Read the paragraph below and use it to answer the following questions.

Child labor exists in two-thirds of the world's nations. From Indonesia to Guatemala, poor children as young as six are sent off to work. Often they are mistreated and punished for not working hard enough. Children mix the gunpowder for firecrackers in China and knot the threads for carpets in India, all for pennies a day. Sometimes they are sold as slaves.

---

1. What is an example of dangerous work done by a child?

    a. stitching a soccer ball

    b. knotting carpet threads

    c. mixing gunpowder

    d. none of the above

2. Which country uses child labor?

    a. China

    b. India

    c. Guatemala

    d. all of the above

3. When young children are forced to work,

    a. they never see their families.

    b. they work but never get paid.

    c. they are punished if they do not work hard.

    d. they are always sold as slaves.

4. Child labor is most common in

    a. countries that make firecrackers.

    b. poor countries.

    c. countries that have slavery.

    d. countries that make carpets.

5. The children who work are often

    a. treated well.

    b. paid generously.

    c. misused.

    d. all of the above

Whole Story Comprehension

Directions: Read the story below and answer the questions on the following page.

Goal: Ending Child Labor

Carefully guiding a needle that's longer than his tiny fingers, a young boy in Pakistan stitches together the leather pieces of a soccer ball. He sits crouched in the corner of a hot, airless shed for 12 hours. For his long day's work, he will earn 60 cents.

The boy is one of more than 200 million children who work at hard, sometimes dangerous jobs all over the world. Child labor exists in two-thirds of the world's nations. From Indonesia to Guatemala, poor children as young as six are sent off to work. Often they are mistreated and punished for not working hard enough. Children mix the gunpowder for firecrackers in China and knot the threads for carpets in India, all for pennies a day. Sometimes they are sold as slaves.

In a speech to the Child Labor Coalition, U.S. Secretary of Labor Robert Reich expressed gratitude for the organization's work to end abuse of child labor, "You turned up the heat, and you got results." He also congratulated Craig Kielburger, 13, of Canada, who traveled the world for a year fighting for kids' rights. Craig believes kids can make a difference. He offers this advice, "Write letters to companies and government officials. Put pressure on leaders to make changes and to stop the misuse of children."

One solution to the child-labor problem in poor countries is education. "The future of these countries," Secretary Reich declared, "depends on a work force that is educated. We are prepared to help build schools."

Education is helping to make the world a brighter place for 12-year-old Aghan of India. When he was nine, Aghan was kidnapped from his home and sold to a carpet maker. Aghan's boss was very cruel. "I was always crying for my mother," he recalls. Aghan's dream was to learn to write so that he could send letters to his parents. Earlier this year, a group that opposes child labor rescued Aghan from the factory. Today, he is living in a shelter in New Delhi and is hard at work learning to write.

Whole Story Comprehension *(cont.)*

Directions: After you have read the story on the previous page, answer the questions below.

1. When children are used to work for unfair wages in poor working conditions, it is best described as
   a. an abuse of working children.
   b. hard work.
   c. a poor working environment.
   d. unfair labor practices.

2. Child labor exists in _____ of the nations of the world.
   a. half
   b. less than half
   c. more than half
   d. all

3. According to the article, children who work under poor conditions
   a. start to work only after age 13.
   b. start to work only after age 12.
   c. make only 60 cents an hour.
   d. may make only 60 cents a day.

4. According to the article, what is the best way to keep many children from falling victim to the abuse of child labor in the future?
   a. Help poor countries educate their children.
   b. Refuse to buy products made in countries that abuse child labor.
   c. Rescue each child.
   d. none of the above

5. Why do families allow young children to go to work?
   a. They don't know how bad it is.
   b. The grownups don't want to work.
   c. The families are very poor and need the income.
   d. The children are paid a lot of money.

6. How do you know Aghan was not happy making carpets away from his family?
   a. He dreamed of learning to write.
   b. He was rescued.
   c. He cried for his mother.
   d. He lives in a shelter.

7. Today in New Delhi, Aghan is
   a. working for a group that is opposed to child labor.
   b. receiving an education.
   c. living with his family.
   d. making carpets.

8. Before you buy a product, how can you tell where a product is made?
   a. Check the label.
   b. Contact the Child Labor Coalition.
   c. Ask the store owner.
   d. Call the company.

Enrichment

Directions: Read the information below and use it to match the meaning with the word.

One way to get a country to change its treatment of child labor is to "boycott" the products that use children to manufacture it. Thus, if we wanted to stop Pakistan from using children to make soccer balls, we would say that we were not going to buy any soccer balls made in Pakistan. A *boycott* is a refusal to deal with something. The term comes from a man in Ireland who was so mean to the people who rented land from him that the neighbors refused to talk to him.

Words sometimes come from the names of people. The *saxophone*, the musical instrument, was invented by Adolphe Sax. A *watt*, a unit of power, was named by the 18th century Scottish inventor, James Watt. *Braille*, the raised writing system used by the blind, is named after its inventor, Louis Braille. A *mentor*, a loyal and wise advisor, comes from Mentor, the trusted friend to Odysseus in Homer's *The Odyssey*.

Other words come from place names. A *hamburger*, the kind you eat with ketchup and French fries, is named after a city in Germany, Hamburg. *Bedlam*, which means crazy or chaotic, comes from the name of a very famous London hospital for the insane. *Denim*, the heavy cotton cloth used for blue jeans, is named for Nimes, France, where it was first woven. *Cashmere*, a very fine wool from mountain goats used for sweaters, scarves, and coats, is from Kashmir in northwestern India. And *gauze*, the loosely woven cloth found in bandages, originated in Gaza in the Middle East.

Words

1. bedlam   _____

2. boycott   _____

3. Braille   _____

4. cashmere   _____

5. denim   _____

6. gauze   _____

7. hamburger   _____

8. mentor   _____

9. saxophone   _____

10. watt   _____

Meanings

a. an advisor

b. a musical instrument

c. used to make very warm clothing

d. a very strong cotton cloth

e. a food made of fried or broiled ground meat

f. a way for people who cannot see to read and write

g. something to cover a cut or sore

h. a very confused and chaotic situation

i. a way of naming the strength of a light bulb

j. a refusal to buy something in protest

Graphic Development

Directions: Look closely at the map that shows where children are hard at work and what their jobs are. Tell if each statement is "True" (T) or "False" (F) according to the map.

Where Children Are Hard at Work

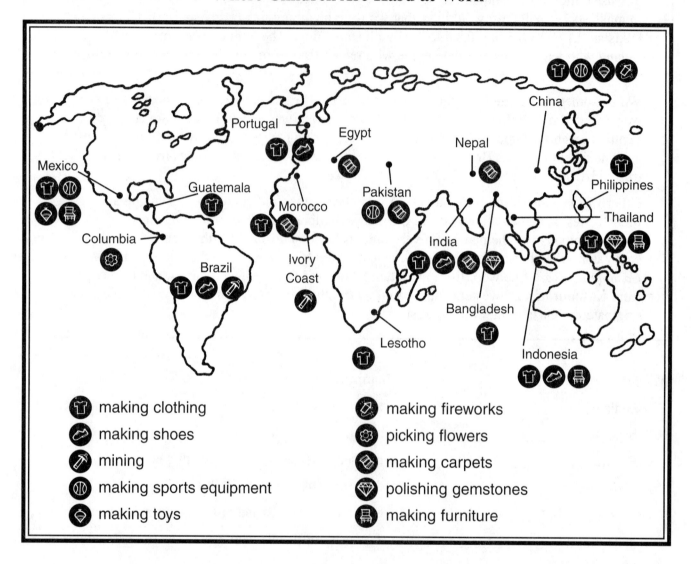

1. Children in Brazil make clothing, work in mines, and make fireworks. _____

2. Children in China make clothing, sports equipment, toys, and shoes. _____

3. Children in Mexico make clothing, sports equipment, and furniture and work in mines.
   _____

4. Children in Mexico, Guatemala, Brazil, Portugal, Morocco, India, Bangladesh, China, Thailand, Indonesia, and the Philippines make clothing. _____

5. Children in the Ivory Coast do not make clothing. _____

Sentence Comprehension

Directions: Read the sentence carefully and use it to answer the following questions "True" (T) or "False" (F).

> Visitors to the western shore of Greenland in July, 1998, may have thought they were dreaming when they saw a Viking ship with a puffy square sail glide past, hugging Greenland's coastline in the icy North Atlantic.

1. The recreation of a Viking ship sailed along the north shore of Greenland. _____

2. People knew it was not an actual Viking vessel. _____

3. Viking ships sometimes used the wind to move. _____

4. Greenland is located in the North Atlantic. _____

5. The date, July, 1998, tells us that the ship the people saw could not be an actual Viking ship. _____

Word Study

Directions: Read the information given below and use it to answer the following questions "True" (T) or "False" (F).

> **Rudder**
>
> It is possible to make a boat go where we want it to go by using sails, paddles, or oars alone, but a *rudder* makes steering a boat easier.
>
> A *rudder* is a flat piece of wood or metal that is attached to the rear of a boat. The rear of the boat is called the stern and the front of the boat is called the bow. When the boat is at rest, the *rudder* sits vertically in the water and protrudes straight out from the rear of the boat.
>
> Today, on large ships, a wheel controls the *rudder*, but in small boats, a tiller is used. The tiller is a piece of wood or some other strong material attached to the top edge of the *rudder*. The tiller allows a sailor to control the *rudder* from inside the boat.
>
> When the boat or ship is under power, either by sail or other means, if the tiller is pushed to the right, the *rudder* moves to the left and the boat's bow will turn to the left. And if the tiller is pushed in the opposite direction, the bow will turn to the right.
>
> A *rudder* is a very important part of a boat or ship.

1. A *rudder* is the same as a tiller. _____

2. A *rudder* is the only object that can steer a boat. _____

3. When the tiller is pushed to the left, the bow of the boat will go to the right. _____

4. Large ships do not need a *rudder*. _____

5. During a trip on a boat, the *rudder* would be wet. _____

Paragraph Comprehension

Directions: Read the paragraph below and use it to answer the following questions.

Eriksson came to North America, which he called Vinland, 1,000 years ago, about 500 years before Columbus. He left from Greenland, home of his father, the explorer, Erik the Red. He went at least as far as Newfoundland, site of the only known Viking settlement in North America. This was the second attempt at the Viking 1000 voyage. A July, 1997, journey ended with the rudder broken. The crew members started this journey in Nuuk, where the previous year's sail ended.

1. Where was the only Viking settlement in North America found?

    a. Sweden

    b. Greenland

    c. Newfoundland

    d. Vinland

2. When did Eriksson explore North America?

    a. about A.D. 1492

    b. about 1,000 years ago

    c. about A.D. 800

    d. a little before A.D. 1000

3. Who was Erik the Red's son?

    a. Leif Eriksson

    b. Robert Stevens

    c. Columbus

4. What Eriksson called Vinland, we call

    a. Greenland.

    b. Canada.

    c. North America.

    d. Norse country.

5. Eriksson sailed from _____ to Newfoundland.

    a. Norway, Denmark, and Sweden

    b. Norse countries

    c. Columbus

    d. Greenland

Whole Story Comprehension

Directions: Read the story below and answer the questions on the following page.

Viking Voyage

Visitors to the western shore of Greenland in July, 1998, may have thought they were dreaming when they saw a Viking ship with a puffy square sail glide past, hugging Greenland's coastline in the icy North Atlantic.

What they really watched was a dream come true. As a child, writer, explorer, and big dreamer, W. Hodding Carter loved to read about the Viking Age, A.D. 800 to 1050. That's when Vikings sailed from the Norse countries of Norway, Denmark, and Sweden for distant lands. Carter asked Maine boatbuilder, Robert Stevens, to build a knarr (pronounced nar), a Viking merchant ship powered by oars and a square sail. In July, 1998, 10 sailors set out to re-create the journey of Viking explorer, Leif Eriksson.

Eriksson came to North America which he called Vinland, 1,000 years ago, about 500 years before Columbus. He left from Greenland, home of his father, the explorer, Erik the Red. He went at least as far as Newfoundland, site of the only known Viking settlement in North America.

This was the second attempt at the Viking 1000 voyage. A July, 1997, journey ended with the rudder broken. The crew members started this journey in Nuuk, where the previous year's sail ended.

Like a giant canoe, a knarr is completely open. The sailors had no shelter from wind, rain, or waves. Most of the time they wore modern sailing gear. However, Carter did wear Viking clothing for a week.

The 1,500-mile journey took over eight weeks. When the wind gave out, crew members rowed. They ate plants and berries gathered ashore, and fish and provisions brought aboard; but the real Vikings had eaten wild seals and walruses.

For safety, Carter and his crew had a radio, compasses, a lifeboat, wet suits, a complete medical kit, and a global positioning system on board. The Vikings tracked their progress by spotting landmarks. On the open seas, they watched for birds as a sign that land was near. At night, they steered by the North Star. Like most people of the time, Vikings believed the earth was flat. Still, they bravely sailed into the unknown.

Whole Story Comprehension (cont.)

Directions: After you have read the story on the previous page, answer the questions below.

1. As a child, W. Hodding Carter was interested in

   a. sailing.
   b. Vikings.
   c. historical reenactments.
   d. boat building.

2. Carter, in an attempt to live like a real Viking,

   a. took no provisions aboard.
   b. fished for food.
   c. ate wild seals.
   d. all of the above

3. Vikings came from

   a. Sweden only.
   b. the Norse countries.
   c. Norway only.
   d. Maine.

4. Whose journey did Carter attempt to re-create?

   a. Erik the Red
   b. Erik Eriksson
   c. Leif Eriksson
   d. A Viking merchant ship

5. Choose the true statement.

   a. Like all Vikings, Carter built his own knarr.
   b. A knarr is a type of boat.
   c. It is known that Leif Eriksson did not go farther than Newfoundland.
   d. W. Hodding Carter only used equipment the Vikings would have used.

6. Unlike the Vikings, Carter and his crew used _____ to guide them.

   a. a global positioning system
   b. landmarks
   c. a rudder
   d. birds

7. How long did the 1,500-mile Viking 1000 voyage take?

   a. eight weeks
   b. two years
   c. 10 days
   d. from A.D. 800 to 1050

8. A knarr is compared to

   a. a Viking merchant ship.
   b. a rowboat.
   c. a sailboat.
   d. a giant canoe.

Enrichment

Directions: Read the information below and use it to match the words with their definitions.

In addition to exploring Greenland and Newfoundland, the Vikings also came to England. One of the oldest poems in English literature is "Beowulf." This poem was first recited orally and finally written down in the tenth century in a language called Old English. It tells of a Swedish hero, Beowulf, who helps a Danish king by killing the monster, Grendel, and his mother. It is not strange that the characters in the poem are from Sweden and Denmark because at that time, the Danes ruled England. King Cnut, a famous English king, was actually a Danish Viking who ruled England from A.D. 1016 to 1035. The Danes were influential in England from A.D. 700 to 1150.

The Scandinavian or Viking influence can also be seen in our English vocabulary, especially in words that begin with "sk-." For example, "sky" and "ski" are of Scandinavian origin. Other words are "skipper" (the captain of a boat or ship), "skull" (the bones of one's head), and "skirt" (as in a woman's skirt). "Skin" is also one of these words. At that time, skins were not only used for clothing, but also as a material on which to write. Our ability to do something easily is called "skill" because of our Viking heritage. We call moving by hops and steps "skipping" because of this heritage. Finally, when we want to wish someone good health, we can say "skoal!"

Words

1. skill   _____
2. skip   _____
3. skirt   _____
4. Beowulf   _____
5. skoal   _____
6. Cnut   _____
7. skull   _____
8. skin   _____
9. Grendel   _____
10. skipper   _____

Definitions

a. a material on which one can write

b. the bones of one's head

c. an early English King

d. the captain of a boat or ship

e. to move by hops and steps

f. an outer garment worn from the waist down

g. an ability to use one's knowledge efficiently

h. a toast wishing someone good health

i. a Swedish hero who kills monsters

j. the son of a monster who attacked the Danes

Graphic Development

Directions: Look closely at the map that shows Leif Eriksson's route and tell if the statements are "True" (T) or "False" (F).

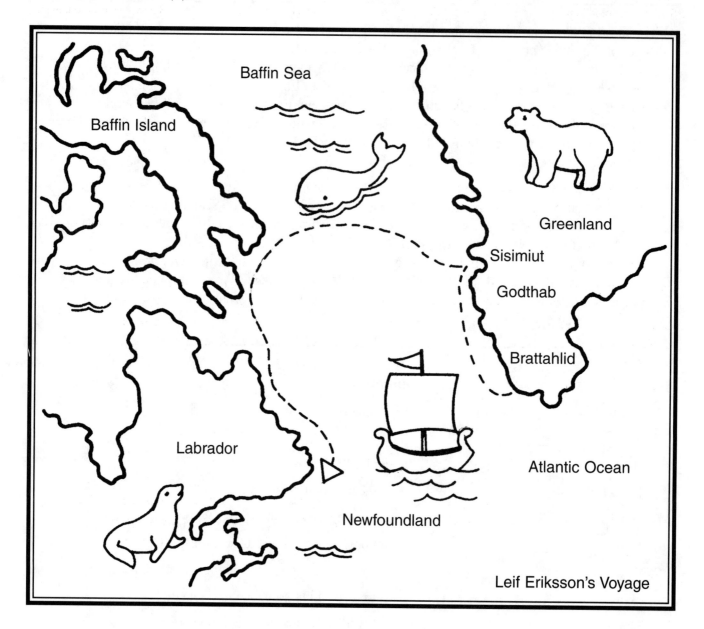

Leif Eriksson's Voyage

1. Polar bears are found in Greenland. _____

2. The knarr has sails. _____

3. Leif Eriksson traveled first north, then east, and finally south. _____

4. Leif Eriksson landed briefly on Baffin Island. _____

5. Brattahlid was Leif Eriksson's destination. _____

Answer Key

Lesson 1

Page 19
Sentence Comprehension
1. F
2. T
3. F
4. T
5. T

Word Study
1. F
2. F
3. T
4. T
5. T

Page 20
Paragraph Comprehension
1. d
2. b
3. d
4. b
5. a

Page 22
Whole Story
Comprehension
1. c
2. a
3. d
4. c
5. b
6. a
7. c
8. a

Page 23
Enrichment
1. No
2. Yes
3. Yes
4. No
5. Yes
6. No
7. No
8. No
9. Yes
10. No

Page 24
Graphic Development
1. F
2. F
3. T
4. F
5. F

Lesson 2

Page 25
Sentence Comprehension
1. F
2. T
3. F
4. F
5. T

Word Study
1. F
2. F
3. T
4. F
5. F

Page 26
Paragraph Comprehension
1. b
2. c
3. c
4. b
5. a

Page 28
Whole Story
Comprehension
1. b
2. b
3. d
4. e
5. a
6. a
7. b
8. c

Page 29
Enrichment
1. Yes
2. Yes
3. Yes
4. Yes
5. No
6. Yes
7. No
8. Yes
9. No
10. No

Page 30
Graphic Development
c. Cleopatra, Queen of the Nile

Lesson 3

Page 31
Sentence Comprehension
1. F
2. F
3. T
4. F
5. T

Word Study
1. F
2. T
3. T
4. F
5. T

Page 32
Paragraph Comprehension
1. d
2. c
3. c
4. c
5. d

Page 34
Whole Story
Comprehension
1. c
2. b
3. b
4. d
5. b
6. d
7. c
8. d

Page 35
Enrichment
1. a
2. b
3. a
4. b
5. c
6. a
7. a
8. a
9. a
10. a

Page 36
Graphic Development
1. C
2. E
3. CE
4. CE
5. CE

Lesson 4

Page 37
Sentence Comprehension
1. T
2. T
3. T
4. F
5. T

Word Study
1. T
2. T
3. F
4. F
5. F

Page 38
Paragraph Comprehension
1. c
2. d
3. b
4. a
5. d

Page 40
Whole Story
Comprehension
1. b
2. c
3. c
4. c
5. d
6. d
7. c
8. d

Page 41
Enrichment
1. e
2. c
3. d
4. d
5. f
6. e
7. a
8. a
9. b
10. b

Page 42
Graphic Development
1. a
2. c
3. e
4. d
5. b

Answer Key (cont.)

Lesson 5

Page 43

Sentence Comprehension
1. F
2. T
3. F
4. F
5. T

Word Study
1. F
2. T
3. T
4. F
5. T

Page 44

Paragraph Comprehension
1. c
2. b
3. a
4. a
5. a

Page 46

Whole Story
Comprehension
1. d
2. b
3. a
4. e
5. b
6. b
7. e
8. c

Page 47

Enrichment
1. d
2. a
3. e
4. b
5. c
6. i
7. h
8. j
9. f
10. g

Page 48

Graphic Development
1. e
2. c
3. f
4. d
5. a
6. b

Lesson 6

Page 49

Sentence Comprehension
1. T
2. F
3. T
4. T
5. F

Word Study
1. F
2. T
3. T
4. T
5. F

Page 50

Paragraph Comprehension
1. c
2. b
3. d
4. c
5. b

Page 52

Whole Story
Comprehension
1. a
2. c
3. b
4. b
5. b
6. a
7. b
8. a

Page 53

Enrichment
1. f
2. e
3. c
4. a
5. g
6. d
7. b

Page 54

Graphic Development
1. i
2. j
3. c
4. f
5. h

Lesson 7

Page 55

Sentence Comprehension
1. T
2. T
3. T
4. F
5. T

Word Study
1. F
2. T
3. T
4. T
5. T

Page 56

Paragraph Comprehension
1. d
2. c
3. c
4. b
5. a

Page 58

Whole Story
Comprehension
1. a
2. b
3. c
4. d
5. b
6. a
7. a
8. c

Page 59

Enrichment
1. N
2. Y
3. N
4. N
5. Y

Page 60

Graphic Development
1. a
2. c
3. b
4. d
5. f

Lesson 8

Page 61

Sentence Comprehension
1. T
2. T
3. F
4. T
5. F

Word Study
1. F
2. T
3. F
4. F
5. T

Page 62

Paragraph Comprehension
1. c
2. a
3. d
4. a
5. b

Page 64

Whole Story
Comprehension
1. b
2. d
3. c
4. d
5. a
6. b
7. a
8. c

Page 65

Enrichment
1. a
2. e
3. f
4. c
5. d
6. f
7. c
8. g
9. c or f
10. f or e

Page 66

Graphic Development
1. d
2. d
3. c
4. a
5. c

Answer Key *(cont.)*

Lesson 9

Page 67

Sentence Comprehension
1. F
2. T
3. F
4. T
5. F

Word Study
1. T
2. T
3. T
4. F
5. F

Page 68

Paragraph Comprehension
1. b
2. b
3. a
4. d
5. a

Page 70

Whole Story
Comprehension
1. d
2. a
3. c
4. d
5. a
6. a
7. d
8. b

Page 71

Enrichment
1. F
2. T
3. F
4. F
5. F
6. F
7. F
8. T
9. T
10. F

Page 72

Graphic Development
1. d
2. e
3. b
4. a
5. c

Lesson 10

Page 73

Sentence Comprehension
1. T
2. F
3. T
4. T
5. F

Word Study
1. F
2. F
3. F
4. T
5. T

Page 74

Paragraph Comprehension
1. b
2. c
3. d
4. a
5. b

Page 76

Whole Story
Comprehension
1. c
2. d
3. b
4. d
5. c
6. a
7. b
8. d

Page 77

Enrichment
1. Y
2. N
3. Y
4. N
5. Y
6. Y
7. Y
8. N
9. N
10. Y

Page 78

Graphic Development
1. e
2. a
3. d
4. c
5. b

Lesson 11

Page 79

Sentence Comprehension
1. F
2. F
3. F
4. T
5. F

Word Study
1. T
2. F
3. T
4. F
5. F

Page 80

Paragraph Comprehension
1. d
2. c
3. a
4. c
5. d

Page 82

Whole Story
Comprehension
1. c
2. b
3. b
4. d
5. d
6. b
7. c
8. b

Page 83

Enrichment
1. h
2. b
3. c
4. m
5. j
6. i
7. n
8. f
9. d
10. a

Page 84

Graphic Development
1. F
2. T
3. F
4. T
5. T

Lesson 12

Page 85

Sentence Comprehension
1. F
2. F
3. T
4. T
5. T

Word Study
1. T
2. T
3. T
4. T
5. F

Page 86

Paragraph Comprehension
1. a
2. c
3. b or a
4. a
5. d

Page 88

Whole Story
Comprehension
1. b
2. a
3. d
4. d
5. b
6. d
7. b
8. a

Page 89

Enrichment
1. F
2. F
3. F
4. F
5. F
6. F
7. T
8. T
9. T
10. T

Page 90

Graphic Development
1. T
2. F
3. F
4. T
5. T

Answer Key *(cont.)*

Lesson 13

Page 91
Sentence Comprehension
1. T
2. F
3. T
4. F
5. T

Word Study
1. N
2. P
3. N
4. P
5. P

Page 92
Paragraph Comprehension
1. a
2. a
3. b
4. d
5. a

Page 94
Whole Story Comprehension
1. a
2. c
3. b
4. a
5. d
6. b
7. d
8. b

Page 95
Enrichment
1. h
2. a
3. b
4. j
5. f
6. d
7. d
8. i
9. g
10. e

Page 96
Graphic Development
1. f
2. c
3. b
4. d
5. f

Lesson 14

Page 97
Sentence Comprehension
1. T
2. F
3. T
4. T
5. F

Word Study
1. F
2. T
3. F
4. F
5. T

Page 98
Paragraph Comprehension
1. d
2. c
3. b
4. d
5. a

Page 100
Whole Story Comprehension
1. b
2. d
3. c
4. a
5. c
6. c
7. b
8. d

Page 101
Enrichment
1. Y
2. N
3. Y
4. Y
5. Y
6. N
7. Y
8. Y
9. Y
10. N

Page 102
Graphic Development
1. c
2. a
3. e
4. b
5. d

Lesson 15

Page 103
Sentence Comprehension
1. T
2. T
3. F
4. T
5. F

Word Study
1. Y
2. N
3. Y
4. Y
5. Y

Page 104
Paragraph Comprehension
1. a
2. b
3. a
4. d
5. d

Page 106
Whole Story Comprehension
1. c
2. c
3. d
4. c
5. d
6. c
7. c
8. a

Page 107
Enrichment
1. b
2. c
3. f
4. i
5. m
6. v
7. a
8. p
9. u
10. j

Page 108
Graphic Development
1. T
2. F
3. T
4. T
5. F

Lesson 16

Page 109
Sentence Comprehension
1. T
2. T
3. T
4. F
5. T

Word Study
1. F
2. T
3. F
4. T
5. F

Page 110
Paragraph Comprehension
1. d
2. c
3. d
4. a
5. a

Page 112
Whole Story Comprehension
1. b
2. b
3. d
4. d
5. b
6. b
7. b
8. d

Page 113
Enrichment
1. F
2. T
3. T
4. T
5. T
6. T
7. F

Page 114
Graphic Development
1. F
2. F
3. T
4. F
5. F

142

Answer Key *(cont.)*

Lesson 17

Page 115
Sentence Comprehension
1. T
2. T
3. T
4. T
5. T

Word Study
1. F
2. F
3. T
4. T
5. F

Page 116
Paragraph Comprehension
1. b
2. c
3. d
4. c
5. b

Page 118
Whole Story
Comprehension
1. c
2. b
3. c
4. d
5. a
6. b
7. b
8. d

Page 119
Enrichment
1. i
2. g
3. b
4. c
5. d
6. h
7. f
8. e
9. j
10. a

Page 120
Graphic Development
1. T
2. F
3. F
4. F
5. F

Lesson 18

Page 121
Sentence Comprehension
1. T
2. F
3. T
4. T
5. T

Word Study
1. T
2. F
3. T
4. F
5. T

Page 122
Paragraph Comprehension
1. c
2. a
3. c
4. a
5. c

Page 124
Whole Story
Comprehension
1. d
2. d
3. a
4. a
5. c
6. d
7. d
8. b

Page 125
Enrichment
1. c
2. b
3. h
4. g
5. f
6. d
7. e
8. j
9. i
10. a

Page 126
Graphic Development
1. F
2. T
3. F
4. F
5. F

Lesson 19

Page 127
Sentence Comprehension
1. F
2. T
3. F
4. F
5. F

Word Study
1. F
2. T
3. F
4. T
5. F

Page 128
Paragraph Comprehension
1. c
2. d
3. c
4. b
5. c

Page 130
Whole Story
Comprehension
1. a
2. c
3. d
4. a
5. c
6. a or c
7. b
8. a

Page 131
Enrichment
1. h
2. j
3. f
4. c
5. d
6. g
7. e
8. a
9. b
10. i

Page 132
Graphic Development
1. F
2. F
3. F
4. T
5. T

Lesson 20

Page 133
Sentence Comprehension
1. F
2. F
3. T
4. T
5. T

Word Study
1. F
2. F
3. T
4. F
5. T

Page 134
Paragraph Comprehension
1. c
2. b
3. a
4. c
5. d

Page 136
Whole Story
Comprehension
1. b
2. b
3. b
4. c
5. b
6. a
7. a
8. d

Page 137
Enrichment
1. g
2. e
3. f
4. i
5. h
6. c
7. b
8. a
9. j
10. d

Page 138
Graphic Development
1. T
2. T
3. F
4. F
5. F

Answer Sheet

Directions: Fill in the bubble of the correct answer "a," "b," "c," "d," or "e" on this sheet. If the answer is "True," fill in the "a" bubble, and if the answer is "False," fill in the "b" bubble.

T F	T F	T F	T F